Warfare
by Honor

The Restoration of Honor

A Protocol Handbook

Qaumaniq and Suuqiina

ISBN: 0-9673791-3-X

Indigenous Messengers International
P.O.Box 339
Portland, TN 37148
ndigenus@comcast.net

Design and Layout by Tony Laidig, Healing the Land

Healing the Land (US)	**Healing the Land** (Canada)
P.O. Box 73	1236 55th St.
Scotland, PA 17254	Delta, BC V4M 3K3
Phone: 717-261-1751	Phone: 604-484-4419
Fax: 760-874-9874	Fax: 760-874-9874

info@healingtheland.com
www.healingtheland.com

For Worldwide Distribution

TABLE OF CONTENTS

TABLE OF CONTENTS

(CONTINUED)

QAUMANIQ'S
ACKNOWLEDGMENTS

WADO to Yahweh, my Creator....Yeshua, my redeemer, and Ruach Ha Kodesh, my helper.

To my husband, Suuqiina, who first introduced me to the concept of protocol, I am so grateful for your spiritual insights, your incredible ability as a writer and the hard work you were willing to do to bring this book together. What an adventure to share my life with such a passionate and challenging man. I love you.

To my children: Anthony, Derrick, Andrea and Daniel. You are the greatest protocol gift the Creator has ever given to me. You are all so uniquely gifted, so wise, so much fun and so forgiving. I am so proud of each one of you. I love you.

To my grandchildren: Cody, Francis, Austin, Scott Jr., Katherine, Rob, Lacey, Kaletia, Joshua, Talley, Lexie, Allie,

Riley, Savannah, Malachi, Athena, Kielee, Harmony Blue, Kymbrena and those yet to come; you are the delight of my heart. I am so proud of each of you. Your hugs and kisses heal me. You give me hope for the future. I love you.

To my children and grandchildren "in love" that married into our unique family: Kim, Chad, Liz, Sarah and those yet so come. You make our family complete. We need you and love you. I am so glad that Yahweh grafted us together. I love you.

To my mother, Rosemary: you are the most gifted teacher I have ever known. You taught me the joy of reading and encouraged me to be a writer. You are an incredible mother and my wonderful friend. You have always been the wind beneath my wings. I love you.

To our extended family: Dwight and Kimberly Jarratt, Scott and Shelley Switzer, Debbie, Matthew, Jonathan and Hannah Davenport: you are my family of choice. We would not have survived without your wisdom, love and sacrifice. You have been Yeshua to us, not just in word, but in deed. I can't imagine life without you. I love you.

To Arni and Yonit Klein and their children Jon, Leanne and Stephanie: you are my Israeli Family... The most generous people I have ever known. I stepped into my destiny when I met you. Partnering with you has been the greatest ride of my life. I love you.

SUUQIINA'S
ACKNOWLEDGMENTS

Quyana to our great King and Author of the Universe, Yahweh. We bless You by the power of the Ruach Ha Kodesh and in the name of Your Son Salvation (Yeshua).

To Qaumaniq (Keeper of the Flame). You have been adopted by the Inuit and given one of our beautiful names. You changed your name, legally, to fully identify with me and my people. What a tremendous gift it is and what great courage it took! Quyana for all that you are! I am so blessed by you and I love you.

Qaumaniq has mentioned many people by name whom I will not duplicate here but acknowledge their significance and my devotion to them all. I add my natural father and his wife, Herman and Lori Smith, who Qaum found just before Christmas of 2003. Herman and Lori, I am blessed to reconnect after 52 years and look forward to many years of mutual fellowship and great joy. To my natural brother Paul and Charlotte Brodin, my sister Geri and Jim DiLuccio, and my sister Casandra, I am delighted to call you family and be able to enjoy your fellowship from time to time. I love you all.

There are many, many people and friends from my "past" life who remain in my memory and heart, too many to begin to mention. Quyana for all your contributions and expressions of support and love throughout the years.

Quyana to the Lincoln family of White Mountain, Alaska who took me in and loved me until it was time to go to the orphanage. I can still remember our first meeting, our fish camp, Camp Hammer, Abraham and Lucy and our little but cozy village. I miss you all and hope to return many times.

Quyana to many Alaska natives who have helped me reconnect since returning to live and work in Alaska. Your kindness and welcome touches my heart. I love the place of my birth and the uniqueness of my heritage, both native and non-native. For all these and much, much more, I give a hearty Quyana (thank you) and hope this book will reflect your contributions to my life and the affections of my heart for you all.

FROM US BOTH

To our friends: Jon and Tami Belcher, Anita Wilson, Jim and Carol Jobe, Jim and Melaine Robinson, Steve and Susan Nichols, Ken and Connie Shaw, Tim and Jaki Denning, Mike and Melody Morris, Paul and Naomi Belts, Richard and Kimberley Nunez, Lonnie and Leanne Satterly, Doyle and Dani Baggett, Jack and Lee Brown, Joanne Brandon, Ann Bell, Cliff Capehart, Steve and Sonya Springer, Clay and Karen Harper, Nancy Oury, Maury and Ann Buchanan, Ken and Christine Hershey, Anita Wilson, Solomon and Madeline Lopez, Yari and Lisa Siltamaki and Carlos Soto. You are the greatest friends and support system in the world. People are fortunate to have one or two friends and we have been blessed with all of you. You have housed us, fed us, prayed for us, mourned with us, and rejoiced with us. You are people of integrity and your lives reflect your love for Yeshua.

To Our Family in Ministry: Breck and Cathy Wilson, Don and Sharon Wiens, Graham and Mary Harvey and the gang at

Crossroads Fellowship, Matthew and Sherrie Moore and the gang at Common Thread, Jim and Diana Wilson, Ron and Sonya Self, Father Chuck and Seiko Mitchell and the gang at St. Judes Episcopal, Eric and Cindy Sandros, Larry and Cathy Russell and the gang at Father's House, Darren and Loraine Williams, Steve and Debbie Eayrs, Sally Fisher, Marlene Herty, Lloyd and Sussane Woleslagle, Danny and Cindi English, Edith Farmer, Dr. Andre and Evelyn Van Mol, Judy Woltemann and the Cincinatti Transformation Group, Barry and Laura Phillips, Gridley Women's Aglow, Rabi Jeff and Marion Weis, Flo and Terry Rennaker, Tom and Lenni Rennerath, Rabi Eric and Barb Carleson, Rose Marie Hanks, W.R. Bentler, John Stoltz, the Glissons, Nick and Diana Gililia, Bill and Leatha Williams, Annie Mattheson, Jeremy and Tiffany Mansfield, Rabi Joseph and Pat Caulfield, Stewart and Marie LeBow, Ken and Linda Parker at Thunderbay, Linda Jabas and the gang at East Gate Church in Homer Alaska. What an awesome group of people you are. You have been so generous with us in prayer support, in finances, and in opening your church families to us. We are so grateful that you are real people who are committed to build relationship with us. You are Kingdom builders. We love you.

To our First Nations Family: Grand-Chief Lynda Prince, Richard and Katherine Twiss, Terry and Bev LeBlanc, Chief Will and Yvonne Mayo, Chief Anne Richardson, John and Paula Sanford, Fern Noble, Mary Glazier, Chief Kenny and Louise Blacksmith, Ken and Martha Gilbert, Jeni and Dave Covil, Doug and Gloria Yates, Dean And Rita Bear Gray, Kris and Elizabeth Jensen, Dewey and Terri Kirstein, Jonathan and Linda Maracle, Jakob and Jodi Trevizno, Gary and Jane Foster, Randy and Edith Woodley, Shirley Frisbee, Shinwauk, Chief Dave and Ingrid

Acknowledgments

Baker, Chief Red Kirby, Clayton Ivey, Art Begay, Kuzin Bruce, Betty Etukuk, Dan and Cyndi LaPlante, Raeline Gladeau, Kyle and Marsha Taylor, Michele and Dave Clark, Thomas and Joni Drake, Don and Mary Gentry, Leon Siu, Yossi and Kuulei Johnson, Allison Shaw, Melba Eads, Lee and Morningstar Aviles, Susan Beaureguard, Tony and Deborah Laidig, Spyder and Tekakwitha Webb, John and Gail Egnew, Tom and Cathy Benzler, Sonny and Mindy Cummins, Ray and Joanne Shelton, Jon and Tawana Lansa, Jerry and Lara Eaglefeather, John and Gerri Grosvenor, Ray and Liz Levesque, Nonnie Smith, Jeff Brogin, Johnny and Julie Violsbos, Dan and Rhoda Mosley, Elmer and Monica, Jerry and Leslie Chapman, Al and Joyce Anderson and so many others too vast to name. You have accepted us into our long lost family. You have been our teachers. We are amazed at your resilience and your ability to rebuild your lives. You have such wisdom. You are the greatest comedians we have ever known. We love our conferences that serve as family reunions for our First Nations family. We are honored to be one of you. You make us proud and we love you.

To our friends, designers and printers of our materials, Tony and Deb Laidig: thank you so much for your hard work, inspiration, patience, understanding, and dedication to all First Nations authors. You're on the front edge of a huge blessing and many books will follow from many sources, all a lasting blessing.

Last but not least to our granddaughter Allie Nicole, our friends Hannah Baggett, Ken Fisher, Deborah and Meagan Conklin, and Don North, all who are now with Yahweh in the great cloud of witnesses, watching over us, and cheering us toward the finish line. Thank you for being family and friends to us. We'll see you soon.

Warfare by Honor

INTRODUCTION

They came, these two, with intentions that were honorable, indeed sacred. They had traveled far and taken risks anyone could respect. They brought a message with them, a good message about a good way. For them, their mission was divine.

A member of the king's court came and ushered them into the presence of the king who was accompanied by the representatives of the royal court and family members. The scene was glorious in the splendor of a foreign culture with its colorful regalia, sensational music, and beautiful language. These indigenous people were not savages, nor barbarians, nor were they godless. They were simply unfamiliar to these foreign guests.

With the rumble of drums, the blowing of horns, the motion of the dancers, and the majesty of the court, these messengers entered the palace of an honorable king and his influential kingdom.

The king motioned for them to approach the throne. They bowed before him and presented their gifts to him. They were led to seats prepared beforehand for them. Upon being seated these messengers crossed their legs revealing the bottoms of their feet to the king. The king immediately stood and left the palace room. His royal court followed him. The messengers were escorted to their temporary residence and soon were compelled to leave the country. As they sailed away from their first assignment, both of these men were perplexed and grieved by the confusion that reigned in their minds and hearts. Had their Creator failed them? Where was His presence when they needed Him most? Had they failed their Creator? Had they been fools?

Every culture of the world has their own taboos—those things they find offensive to them. Every culture has a protocol or a way of doing things they find affirming and supportive of their customs. Every culture has a right to have these customs and traditions. Cultural practices are the cement that holds the people within the boundaries of their identity. These taboos, protocols, customs, and traditions ought to be explored by those who wish to enter and/or influence that culture. Here is where the messengers had made their mistake. They had not studied the culture before they arrived. They had come as speakers instead of listeners thus not taking the time to find out the taboos that might offend their hosts.

Most cultures find certain gestures offensive. Gestures can signal an intention that could be interpreted as friendly, or arrogant, or even completely antagonistic. In the Western culture, a raised middle finger is a gesture of extreme dishonor. In the story of the messengers, the showing of the bottoms of their feet displayed a similar dishonor.

Introduction

In the case of this nation, the messengers involved, and because of the offense that occurred, the message of the gospel was not allowed into that country for twenty-five years. A simple understanding of protocol might have changed the whole story and a good report might have been handed down as an illustration of "what to do" instead of "what not to do." (We wrote this true story with information added for dramatic effect but the point of the story still haunts those messengers and their supporters.)

In this handbook, we attempt to persuade the reader to begin a process whereby the protocols, the traditions, the customs, and the taboos are carefully examined before attempts are made to influence cultures other than one's own. Since the Creator made the cultures, every culture is worthy of respect, honor, and understanding. A thorough knowledge and careful personal preparation about the culture being visited should be a foundational value common to all professing to know and follow the Creator.

For the sake of the length of the book, we have limited our examples. No single book could hold the vast array of beautiful and meaningful protocols available to us. Since there are thousands of ways to honor people and their ways, we have compiled a short list of examples to help us get started, to become inspired, and maybe to repent of times when offences were committed. We pray that honor will be restored to the believing community.

Many of our examples use First Nations people and their customs (First Nations refer to both the American and Canadian indigenous people also called aboriginal, native, indigenous or host people of the land). Chief Sitting Wind of the Stoney Nation said, "I hope that everyone becomes more sympathetic and less judgmental of us Indians. We have suffered and continue to suffer. It is as if we are trying to climb a falling tree….a strong one which my ancestors grew up with and completely trusted for centuries."[1]

The tree may have fallen but it is worth replanting it. We are "trying to climb." The goal may be above us but it is not beyond reach of anyone's desire to be a person of honor. "The day will come when Indians will not be concerned with struggling for their basic civil rights only, but for the basic rights of all individuals."[2] For a person to be considered and treated as a person of honor is a basic right for all people of the world.

The power of protocol has not been lost so much as it has been ignored. It's power has neither been lost nor ignored by specific elements of society, ie.; diplomats for whom protocol is the most significant and necessary component in governmental representation, for the scientific and medical world where protocol can be the difference between discovery and endless search or even between life and death, for the indigenous native community where protocol is one of the last links to their honorable traditions and the integrity of their culture which continues to be besieged by the forces of assimilation.

Protocol is ignored by the general population where the order and established priority that describe it is publicly denied but secretly admired. The longing for such order and priority is returning and being sought by many.

There was a time in history when protocol was the rule of the day. Countries were governed by strong, centralized powers, and honor was held in high esteem from its loftiest king to the humblest peasant. Later in history, republic governments and liberated societies overthrew the protocol along with the monarchies.

Sometimes, protocol is used by politicians or others to stage events to manipulate impressions rather than to convey meaningful and lasting honor for those deserving of it. It is a sham and we all know it and many find it disgusting. Our children are asking for its restoration by adopting protocol's power through gangs, cultural rules of conduct, dress or regalia, and hierarchy. Do we have something to offer them? Is it possible for our generation to restore the power of protocol or shall we leave it to the next?

Protocol helps society understand the difference between those who have authority and those who merely claim to have it. It allows for genuine differences to exist between chiefs and non-chiefs. Protocol is what keeps distinction or place from degenerating to a caste system or an opportunity for oppression. It allows chiefs to convey their wishes and dreams for their people. It allows the people to address grievances and seek justice with the chiefs. It effectively neutralizes paternalism.

Protocol insists on maintaining the dignity or honor of a person or group of people no matter what their place may be. Protocol is the voice of honor. If protocol is lost or ignored, the voice has been silenced. In North America, the voice is being heard again but the language is unfamiliar to most. It is the language of the heart and not the head.

Protocol is not simply etiquette or manners but it includes them. Protocol is doing what is right between people. It is about honor, dignity, place, space, history, achievement, wisdom and caring.

Warfare by Honor

Honor wears many faces. There is honor that is hard earned such as our public servants who put themselves in harm's way for our safety. There is honor given as recognition of a place, a people, or a culture that is intrinsically present. There is honor given as a simple gift such as, "it is an honor to have you in our home." There are endless layers of honor and honoring available to serve anyone desiring to become a person of honor.

Where there are significant racial, economic, social, and educational disparities, the root cause is generally the loss of willingness to give honor where it is due. Honor is always a pro-active thing. To simply stop dishonoring someone isn't the same as giving them honor. Honor takes creativity, time, and hard work. It may mean sacrificing some things that are quite dear to one's life.

Within everyone there are wars over right and wrong, good and bad, arrogance or compassion, prejudice and inclusion, and honor and dishonor. These wars are evidence that we are alive, really alive and therefore must make choices that affect our own lives and those of others. When someone arrives at the inner war of honor versus dishonor, we are encouraging a choice for *warfare by honor*.

NOTES ON THE USE OF
BIBLICAL NAMES

In this handbook we use the name Yahweh for "God" simply because that is His name while "God" is simply a description. It is honorable to use His name in a good way. We also use other biblical names such "El Elyon," "Adonai," etc.

We use the name Yeshua for the usual name "Jesus." Yeshua is his Hebrew name and the name by which he was known in his own land. We are not legalistic about this usage but it seems honorable to us to use his cultural name. More details are given in the chapter on names.

Some uses of the word "church" are to mean the religious system that professes a form of Christianity or religion, not the true believers, called out ones, or Bride of Yeshua.

Warfare by Honor

Chapter One

Honor

"Honor is the native language of heaven."[1]

Fawn Parrish

"Honor all people."

I Peter 2:17

In his book *The Gift of Honor*, Gary Smalley says that "Honor is a decision we make to place high value, worth and importance on another person by viewing him or her as a priceless gift and granting him or her a position in our lives worthy of great respect; and love involves putting that decision into action."[2]

To honor someone is to give them weight or importance in our lives. When we dishonor people we treat them lightly and with little value.

When we value a person lightly, it seems that we can justify treating that person in dishonorable ways. This is often the case in child abuse, animal cruelty, polluting of the land, domestic violence, and racism. In order to correct these problems we must get to the root of the problem. That problem is the lack of honor.

"Dishonor can not be the gospel."

Fawn Parrish shares in her book on *Honor* that there are three levels of honor spoken of in the scriptures that apply to man. "Intrinsic honor is the first and is the honor that Yahweh gives to everyone. The second level of honor is based on character and the third level of honor is based on performance. She adds that the essence of Yahweh is honor and He is honor personified."[3] Satan, on the other hand, personifies dishonor.

If this is true, and it is, we have to admit that many times in our religious zealousness and our human natures, we have been operating dishonorably toward others. We could not have been operating in the power of the Ruach Ha Kodesh (Holy Spirit). His Spirit would not be dishonorable. This realization made me rethink some of what I had been taught about the bringing of the gospel to the indigenous peoples of the world. If their land was stolen, their people killed, and their cultures were destroyed, as they were, then it could not have been the true gospel. Dishonor cannot be the gospel.

What would happen if each person decided to become a person of honor? How would our homes, our schools, our work places and our churches change. I believe we would see not just change but transformation. We would see such transformation that Yeshua could habitate with us instead of visiting us from time to time.

Honor

The act of honor is not something that we add on with good intentions. It is foundational. It is a building block that is solid and will hold us in the storms that are to come. Our relationships will be shaken but if we are radically committed to honor, it will guide and guard our steps.

In the native culture there are four basic values of the people. The first is reverence, the second is respect, the third is peace, and the fourth is honor. The highest of these four is honor. Honor is integrity in its highest form. In the native marriage ceremony the man vows, "I give you my life and my honor." The woman answers, "I accept your life and your honor and shall treat it as my own."[4] To be honorable and to hold another person's honor as ones own is the greatest promise that can be given.

To be a person of honor in our society is not an easy task. It takes effort. It can be extremely sacrificial as described in this story. Some time back we attended the Gathering of All Nations in Ottowa. A group of leaders from Kansas were also attending and it was their first time to experience a protocol ceremony with the First Nations people. Alyssa describes her experience as follows:

"Before each service during the Gathering of Nations, protocol took place. It did not matter if it ate up the worship time, we still worshipped. It did not matter if it took all the time the speaker was supposed to have, the speaker still spoke. But it did matter that protocol took place and the people were duly honored for their service to the Lord and to one another. During protocol, the people who serve are gifted with beadwork, artwork, music, musical instruments, scarves, etc. But these weren't presents that had been bought in a hurry and lugged to the conference just in case somebody needed a present. No, the First Nations people give away the things that are very dear to them so that the person they are honoring knows they have been blessed and honored from the depths of one's heart. These gifts are gifts that have been made by the hands of the givers or their families, or have been bestowed on them in honor. They have deep personal value.

Many chiefs, warriors, gatekeepers, and humble servants were honored throughout the weekend. So, when we were asked to come up on the platform to be honored I was surprised. These people had honored us at our festival twice, and we didn't deserve it then, and we especially didn't deserve it at this conference. I don't say that as false humility, I mean it. As the weekend went on, we watched, amazed, as generosity and selflessness repeated itself.

A change began to squeeze my heart when Kenny Blacksmith, a humble, former deputy Grand Chief, who had sacrificed all his finances plus some, to put this gathering on for his native brothers and sisters, to be able to worship together, and Lynda Prince, former GrandChief, decided to honor us too. We may not have truly understood the significance of his gift had the rest of the congregation not gasped when it was presented to three Anglo people. We were lavished with gifts from men and women who had only enough money to get to the conference and had no idea how they were going to get home. We were honored by native leaders living in Alaska where cereal is $10 a box, but they make due on $1,000 a month income. We were honored by people living in villages where no roads exist still today.

One moment of protocol stands out so powerfully in my mind and I hope I never forget it. Sunday morning Kenny gave his speaking platform to a Grand Chief of several tribes in Alaska, Will Mayo. After Will's message, Kenny came up to the microphone and said, "I'd like to honor you, Will." Kenny had a chief's coat handmade of buckskin and lavish beadwork indicative of his tribe. It smelled of many years spent in the village hunting and trapping to feed his family. It smelled of the fires burned to cure the meat and to keep his family warm. And it was beautiful. I knew that coat meant a lot to Kenny. It marked him as a great man in his tribe and only leaders were allowed to wear that chief's coat. Will accepted it by receiving it in a manner worthy of such a gift—he broke into a native dance of humble thanks. The dance was as beautiful as the coat.

Then something else happened. As Will told us later, God had already asked him while he was traveling to Canada if he was truly willing to let go of all his treasures to serve Him and Will said. "Yes of course." "Even your Chief's Coat?" "Yes, Lord, even my Chief's Coat. I would give that up." But Will hadn't thought that he would actually have to. When Kenny placed his buckskin jacket on Will's shoulders, Will knew God was calling his bluff. Will stood up, with his Alaskan chief's coat and came over to Kenny. We all watched—a great hush had come over the whole room. I was sitting near Will's wife as he began to explain how she had made this coat for him, how the elder's in the village had been commissioned to lay the beadwork according to tradition for a chief. There were thousands and thousands of beads sewn on that buckskin, lined with fur, and people from thousands of miles around him knew him as a great Chief by his coat. Will handed the coat to Kenny to show his appreciation for the serving and gentle heart Kenny is so well-known for. People were crying softly. I watched Will's wife cry, and took in the significance of the sacrifices these people were making in order to respect and create unbreakable bonds of love. Not only did they sacrifice all the money they had in order to be able to come together to worship Jesus Christ, they wrestled with their own flesh and clinging to earthly symbols and prestige and power. I watched as these people let it go. I watched as these things were replaced with the Spirit of God, with a great and powerful love, and a genuine humility that held more power than any of the sermons I had heard. I watched as these people took all of God they could hold and let it fill them. They gave everything, and the joy in it filled the room. And when we were all leaving, gifts in tow, I saw how a giving heart is doubly blessed. Not only were these selfless people given double what they had given away, they left with a fuller heart, spiritual renewal. My hope is that I will take this message of protocol with me and live it out as generously as I have witnessed it."[5]

Honor moves our hearts. It moves us when we receive it and it moves us even more powerfully when we give it to others. It especially moves a pre-believing world to witness the process take place. It is inspired by the Godhead who lived to protocol/honor one another. The Father honored His son, Yeshua honored His Father and we are to honor both through lives of obedience and worship. How can we say we have the Spirit and not have honor?

Where do we begin? We begin here, by first admitting that we are wanting in this area. We have all but lost the essence of honor in our generation. There was a time it was polite to say "Yes Maam" and "No Maam" as an acknowledgement of elder-ship. There was a time people would stand when an elder, pastor or teacher entered the

"To honor we must be purposeful and deliberate in our actions."

room. There was a time when children had a healthy fear of disobeying parents. There was a time ...that time has long since departed. The freedom of the sixties and seventies took with them the freedom of respect and honor. The price we paid as a generation, to throw off restraint, incurred a debt which our children and grandchildren are paying.

Can we repair the damage? I believe that we can. We must fight to restore that value of honor to our heirs. It is an inheritance that they deserve to own. We can do it if we are willing to be pro-active. Honor does not happen by simply refraining from dishonoring others. To honor we must be purposeful and deliberate in our actions.

We must look for ways to rebuild the walls that have been broken down. It is not too late.

Warfare by Honor

Alaska Native- Ways Of Honor

- *Show Respect to Others*
- *See Connections - All Things Are Related*
- *Honor Your Elders - They Show You The Way Of Life*
- *Accept What Life Brings - You Cannot Control Many Things*
- *Have Patience - Some Things Cannot Be Rushed*
- *Pray For Guidance - Many Things Are Not Known*
- *Live Carefully - What You Do Will Come Back To You*
- *Take Care Of Others - You Cannot Live Without Them*
- *Share What You Have - Giving Makes You Richer*
- *Know Who You Are - You Are A Reflection Of Your Family*[6]

Chapter Two

The First Step of Protocol
The Recognition of Boundaries

Without the recognition of boundaries protocol is not possible. We cannot honor a boundary that we do not know exists. I believe that boundary work is one of the most crucial works that we can do in the Kingdom and it has been sorely overlooked.

As a former counselor, most of the problems that the people brought to me had to do with boundary problems. In our world today, we have not been taught the importance of boundaries and the importance of being people who honor boundaries in ourselves and for others.

Yahweh is a God of boundaries and He establishes boundaries.

Warfare by Honor

The God who made the world and all things in it, since He is the Lord of heaven and earth, does not dwell in temples made by hands; nor is He served by human hands, as though He needed anything, since He Himself gives to all people life and breath and all things; and he made from one man every nation of mankind to live on the face of the earth, having determined their appointed times and the boundaries of their habitation, that they would seek God, if perhaps they might find Him, though He is not far from each of us (see Acts 27:17-18).

Psalm 16:6 says, "The boundary lines have fallen to me in pleasant places; indeed, my heritage is beautiful to me."

Deut.27:17 says, "Cursed is he who moves his neighbor's boundary mark."

"Boundaries define us, what is me and what is you. They show me where I begin and where someone else begins. They also show what is mine, what is yours, and in so doing let us know what is under our stewardship. Without boundaries there is chaos and lawlessness."[1]

When Yahweh told Adam and Eve that they could eat of all the trees in the garden but one, He was establishing a boundary for them. When the children of Israel were given the Torah on Mt. Sinai, He was establishing boundaries for them. These commandments (laws) were a father's instructions for his children and He told them that keeping these commandments would bring them life. To disobey those commandments would bring them death. When we encroach on someone else's boundary or on Yahweh's boundary, we sin. Yahweh takes this very seriously and so should we.

The Scriptures clearly tell us what our boundaries are to be and how to protect them. When He says, in Proverbs, "to watch the path of our feet, to guard our hearts and minds, to let our eyes stay fixed on Him," He is defining for us boundary markers for our personal lives.

Then the Lord God formed man out of dust from the ground (see Gen. 2:7).

Therefore we are dirt or land that needs to be healed and restored to His original purposes.

Boundaries help us identify our property so that we can steward and take care of it. Boundaries are

"In order to understand why we should practice protocol, we need to first acknowledge what boundaries are and how to establish them."

℘

like fences to keep the good in and the bad out. Our personal decisions about who we are, what we want, and what we will allow are the gates in those fences. If we erect impregnable walls where nothing can go in and out, we become isolated and toxic like a stagnant pond.

Boundaries are established by Yahweh Himself. Yahweh defines Himself in a very concrete way. He says that He is love and that there is no darkness in Him (see 1 John 4:16). He tells us what He thinks, feels about things, and the consequences of the action He will take if we disobey Him.

In order to understand why we should practice protocol, we need to first acknowledge what boundaries are and how to establish them. What follows is an example of boundaries.

Our Physical Bodies

"Our skin or physical bodies are one of our most fundamental boundaries. The skin keeps germs outside and protects our bodies and bones. It also has openings to let in food and nourishment."[2]

When individuals have been physically or sexually abused, their first line of defense, the skin, has been encroached upon. These forms of abuse teach people untruths about their physical bodies; that their property does not begin at the skin, that others can invade their most personal property and do whatever they want to them. Everyone needs touch but that touch should be consensual and not forced.

In many faiths, the practice of laying on of hands for prayer is done. Those who use this form of prayer should ask the person who is receiving the prayer, "May I touch you?" The same is true with hugs and other forms of showing affection. In many churches the pastor says, "Grab ten people and hug them before you sit down." This pastor is probably well meaning and wants to create an atmosphere of care and affection for the people. What the pastor does not realize is that he/she has just released the people to bash others' boundaries. If a leader instructs his/her people to hug there should be some instruction on proper protocol to honor the boundaries of others by simply asking, "May I give you a hug?" The people should be told that it's perfectly permissible to answer, "No" without the threat of being judged as cold or less spiritual.

As Suuqiina and I travel, we practice boundaries. We do not allow people that we do not know well to lay hands on us. We learned this the hard way when a lady came to pray for us and laid her hands on our genitals. Now, we also keep our eyes open.

We also do not hug people of the opposite sex unless we are well acquainted with them and know they are respectful and honoring people. This is not a rule we are putting on others but a boundary that we have established for our relationship and marriage.

Suuqiina and I travel extensively across North America. A few times we have encountered people who want to express affection and touch in an inappropriate way. On two occasions I talked to women who I felt had touched my husband in a way that felt defiling to me. On one occasion, a woman grabbed him and brought him into her chest for a frontal hug. It was quite a spectacle to watch him try to squirm away while she held him in a choke- hold. I went to the woman later and told her that I did not wish her any harm or shame but that I did not like the way that she had manhandled my husband. She laughed it off with, "Oh honey that's just how I am." I told her, "I do not wish to change you but I want you to know that I expect you not to do that to my husband in the future."

In another situation, a woman grabbed my husband and kissed him before we both could catch a breath. I waited until I had calmed down, from the anger I felt at our boundaries being bashed, before talking to her. In a kind and firm tone I let her know that I did not appreciate her kissing my husband. I told her that kissing is an intimate act for us and that we did not feel comfortable with her expression toward my husband. She told me that she kisses people all the time and that that was just her way. Once again I said, "I am not trying to change you but I am letting you know that your kissing my husband is not o.k. for me and I am asking you not to do it again."

Some might ask, "Why did you speak up instead of your husband?" My answer to that is that husband's speak up for their wives many times. If another man makes a pass at his wife, it is seen as an honorable act for the husband to speak to the offending man and let him know the boundaries concerning his wife. I feel that it is time that women be afforded the same opportunities. Too many women have watched their husbands be carried off before their very eyes while they have waited for their husbands to notice the encroachment. It is time for us, as women, to participate as gatekeepers in our marriages.

Suuqiina and I have also had people in meetings grab us against our will and say, "I know that you said not to hug you but I am a hugger and I am going to hug you anyway." When a person does this, they expose themselves as a boundary basher and not a person of honor. This person is not a safe person and not someone we will bring into our hearts and lives.

People who do not acknowledge boundaries or see the wisdom of them will accuse us of being paranoid or unfriendly. We do not succumb to the manipulation or pressure to put our boundaries aside in order to be liked. Our marriage is much too important to us and is worth protecting.

We have seen people come up to pregnant women and touch their stomachs without permission. We have also seen strangers touch little children they don't know. These acts may seem innocent but they reveal a lack of boundaries on the part of the individuals doing these things.

Our Communication

"Our words are another form of boundaries."[3] My counselor used to say, "'No' is a sentence." This was something that

I needed to learn because I had trouble saying 'no' to others when they would ask something of me. I learned later, through my own recovery process from co-dependency, that my words let people know where I stand and give people a sense of the boundaries around me. If people treated me poorly I needed to give them a clear message, with my words, that their behavior was not o.k.

> *"People with boundary problems in the area of words will sometimes interrupt others without realizing it."*

"People with boundary problems in the area of words will sometimes interrupt others without realizing it. They might also talk incessantly and have trouble listening to others. Our communication skills are very important because our words represent the largest and most consistent boundary we have."[4]

Poor communication skills require us to work at strengthening our verbal boundaries using wisdom, grace, and respect coupled with firmness, resolve, and courage.

Geographical Space

"The geographical distance or space between people is also a boundary. Some people and cultures are more comfortable with a small amount of space between themselves and others, while other cultures feel crowded and encroached upon with physical closeness."[5]

There was a gentleman in my church who used to pick me up, when he hugged me, and twirl me around. I felt very uneasy with this gesture. He would say that he meant nothing by it but a show of affection. For me it felt invasive. When he did not respond to a verbal request to acknowledge my boundary, I made sure that I was not in a position again to be his victim.

I know a gentleman who likes to be one inch from the face of another person when he talks to them. At the same time, while he is talking, he will hold their arm so they cannot move. He seems unaware that he is in the personal space of others. It will come as no surprise that this same man bashes people's spiritual boundaries as well by telling people what they should think and believe about Yahweh.

When it comes to acknowledging the personal boundary space of others, we should give respect to the person who needs the greatest amount of space for their personal comfort. People will give clues that let us know what their geographical boundaries are by backing up, putting out their hand for a hand shake rather than a hug, or putting an object between us and themselves. In order to be honorable, we need to be aware of these signals.

Time

Time is another boundary.

When Suuqiina and I speak at a conference, we thank the people for giving us their time and attention because time is like land. We are only given a certain amount of time in our lives and it is precious to us. When people are late to a commitment or an appointment and they cause others to wait on them, they are stealing from those people. They are encroaching on their lives. We make sure we keep within the time limits that we are given for our speaking time or else we are stealing the next speaker's time.

"Time can also be used as a boundary when we need time off from a person or activity in order to refresh our souls or be renewed."[6]

In the Psalms we are told to "number our days" for the purpose of "applying our hearts to wisdom." Most people don't understand that concept. However, the older one becomes, the more important time inventories become. Time requires the same commitment of stewardship as our health, spiritual growth, and relationships. Take some time and do a personal time inventory and see if there are changes needed and boundaries to be repaired or created.

Money

Our money is a boundary. Where we give our money, invest our money, and spend our money is our business. We should not be coerced in the area of giving, investing, or spending. In order to have a life that is manageable, we will need to have boundaries around our finances.

Money has an odd way of changing people. If people are poor they have distinctly different boundaries than people who are wealthy. Everyone once in awhile you meet some one who is, in all appearances and actions normal, only to find out later they are wealthy. Those exceptions are rare.

I had a mentor once ask what I would do if I were given five million dollars. After some thinking I produced a list of ideas for him. He looked it over and remarked that I would likely not be a recipient of that amount of money as I had no distinct or developed boundaries about money. Money boundaries need to be taken seriously, developed early, and carefully sustained.

Emotional Space

Our emotional space and our emotions are also a boundary for us. We should not let others tell us how to feel or that our feelings are not legitimate. Our feelings are our feelings and are neither good nor bad. "Emotional distance is a temporary boundary that allows us to feel safe."[7] By temporary, I mean that we cannot live in isolation. At some point we must relate to others in our lives.

"Emotional protocol requires that we 'laugh with those who laugh and weep with those who weep.'"

Many men have difficulty in their emotional relationships. One of the best books I've ever read on the subject is *Discovering the Mind of a Women* by Ken Nair. If you laughed at that title you desperately need the book. Emotional space and emotional boundaries are no laughing matter. The Holy Spirit understands women, understands emotions, and has His own boundaries. He can, for instance, be grieved. If you have the Holy Spirit in you, the potential for understanding your wife, daughters, or other women is real and potent. We will be held accountable about our emotional stewardship. Ask yourself, "Have I lived with my wife in an understanding way?" (see 1 Peter 3:7)

The First Step of Protocol

Most men have never taken a personal emotional inventory. They do not know what their emotional boundaries are. Most simply go through life assuming their reactions and responses are correct ones. Not knowing their own emotional boundaries, they are not aware of bashing others' and may not even realize the damage that has been done to those they love.

Emotional protocol requires that we "laugh with those who laugh and weep with those who weep." Ask yourself, "Can I do that?"

Right to Privacy

The right to privacy is also a boundary. We do not have to share personal information with others. It is not right for our private information to be shared with others without our permission, even in the form of prayer requests. That is only a religious way of gossiping.

Just because a pastor or leader is in leadership does not give the congregation the right to know all of the private details of their lives. These families deserve privacy and respect of their personal and family boundaries.

A few years back I put a prayer request on our email list. It seemed harmless enough. I listed all of our children's names on the list for prayer. One of our children called me and asked me not to ever list their name again. They had received a call from a friend of theirs who saw their name listed on the web site and wondered if something was wrong in their lives. Our child said, "If you want to put your name on the internet that is fine but please do not put my name out there. I don't want people to know my private business or to even know that I exist." To our child this act of getting prayer, from what were strangers to them, was intrusive. I had to apologize for disregarding their boundaries by not asking permission. We can learn a lot from our children if we are teachable. The scriptures teach children to "honor their parents" but the assumption is that the parents will be honorable people. Make a commitment to your child to never share anything about them publicly without first checking with them. If you can keep this commitment, you will likely keep their honor for you.

The right to privacy includes "working out your own salvation with fear and trembling." Most believers have let the church or some system do that for them. Your relationship with the Creator is a private one and you have right to share as much or as little as you want to about it. Do not let a mob rule your spiritual life. Work it out and keep it real.

Giftings and Talents

Our gifts and talents are also boundaries in our lives. They are uniquely ours given by God. They are not to be exploited or used by anyone. How many times have we watched extremely gifted people come in to the Kingdom of Yahweh, full of zeal for the Lord, then thrown right in to leadership positions,   due to the gifts that they possess. Sad to say, but many times their gifts take them where their character can't keep them. They allow themselves to be used by a religious system that has little regard for their souls. How tragic this can be for these people and their families.

Another boundary line that is to be drawn is give honor where it is due, in the area of spiritual gifting. Many times people behind the scenes in churches do the hard work and the leadership, out-front people, take the credit. I said "take" the credit because that is what they are doing. It doesn't take much humility to give credit to the people behind the scenes for their contributions.

One thing that Suuqiina and I have purposed to work at is crediting people that have given us revelation, insights, and illumination through their teaching. One of our Board Members, Shelley Switzer, gave us a revelation concerning the restoration of women. When we tell that insight, we make a point of telling the people that the revelation came through Shelley. When we speak about the revelation that we've been given concerning Israel, we say the insight came through Arni and Yonit Klein. Our friend, Fern Noble, gave us the title of this book and when we speak about 'warfare by honor,' we tell people that she coined that phrase. It is against the law to pla-giarize the writings of others, but many people feel they can steal insights without giving credit. It is honorable to give credit to the source of insights, after all it is the truth.

Spirituality

Our spirituality and how we express it is also a boundary. We do not have to express our spirituality like anyone else because we are unique. We should not be forced to be like anyone else. We should not be looked down upon if we are different. What a tragedy it has been for the indigenous peo-ples of the world when the Anglo missionaries took their cul-ture from them. The native cultural expression of worship through instruments, regalia, and native language was seen as demonic and they were told that had to give up their culture to become a Christian. This is such a tragic example of spiritual abuse.

Spiritual abuse can also happen within the confines of church meetings and gatherings. I have been in church meetings where it seemed like a game of 'Simon Says.' The worship leader would yell out commands at the people prodding them to worship. True worship is an act of the heart and cannot be manipulated and should not be forced through threats, pleadings, or any other shame producing activities. Honorable worship leaders make honest invitations, set reasonable boundaries, and let the Holy Spirit move on the hearts of the worshippers.

"True worship is an act of the heart and cannot be manipulated...."

In one service, I saw a woman come across the room and force another woman to raise her hands by holding the woman's hands over her head. It actually interrupted that woman's worship and made her a victim of spiritual abuse.

We have seen the so-called "prophetic" used to control and manipulate people. When our granddaughter died, I was appalled at how many people had 'words' for us that they thought were from the Lord. Some were contradictory with each other and others were cruel and destructive. I knew the people were well meaning but they had little regard for timing or spiritual boundaries.

Honorable prophets can and should invite scrutiny of their 'words' without placing burdens on others to "believe" and "receive" their 'words.' If we "see in part," and we do, and we "know in part," and we do, then we should not fear whatever time or space might be necessary for any prophetic 'word' to find its place in people's lives. No true prophet need fear the time or space necessary for 'words' to take root in the hearts and lives of people. Anything less can be and usually is some form of spiritual abuse.

I believe that the bashing of spiritual boundaries can have the most devastating effect in a person's life. If the representation of Yahweh is used to control and abuse others, where can one run for safety or comfort?

We are the gatekeepers to these areas of our lives and we will be held accountable for how we have stewarded our personal land, how we trespass on the land of others, or take what belongs to them. Remember, we are cursed if we move someone's boundary stone. Where boundaries have not been acknowledged, stewarded and honored, devastation has occurred.

Boundaries are established by Yahweh to protect us. Yahweh would not allow anyone but the High Priest into the Holy of Holies. This protected the people and was not a rule to keep the people away.

In the Old Testament, the temple was a physical building. After Yeshua came, we became the temple where the Lord lives. "Do you not know that you are a temple of Yahweh and that the Spirit of Yahweh dwells in you. If any man destroys the temple of Yahweh, Yahweh will destroy him, for the temple of Yahweh is Holy and that is what you are (see 1 Cor.3:16-17)." We are the gatekeepers of this temple and must be responsible to keep things that defile the temple out, and let the holy things in.

As I said previously, this is not meant to lead you to become reclusive or isolated. We all need touch, love, affection, and attention. We need to share with others and have them share with us. We need to open the doors of our hearts to true Christian fellowship and invite other people into our hearts and lives. However, we must be responsible to whom we open our lives to.

Many people come to Yeshua who have been hurt and have had their personal boundaries bashed. They come expecting to find a sanctuary with Yahweh's people. They come with the mistaken idea that the church is a safe haven for them in which to let down their defenses. This is a false expectation. The church is not a safe place. The Lord is a safe place but the church is not. Many people come into the kingdom with baggage and some are never freed of their baggage until they meet Yeshua face to face. Many come from years of abuse and dysfunction including addiction. Some are not honoring of others and are 'takers' rather than 'givers.' Hurting people come to the church and hurting people, many times, hurt others. We must always be stewards of our lives and practice boundary keeping for ourselves, not expecting others to do it for us.

We cannot come into the house of the Lord and live under the fantasy that everyone in those walls is safe and will honor us. We must grow up and be responsible to oversee our lives and those of our spouses and children. We must be gatekeepers, alert to attacks from the enemy from within the walls of our spiritual houses known as the 'church.' We want to be free to connect with others but we must not throw off all restraint, blindly trusting everyone.

The First Step of Protocol

The residential schools, that the Native American Indians were placed in by the government, are a perfect example of this. These schools, where much of the sexual and physical abuse happened, were operated by the church. There were people in authority there that were not safe. Horrible acts of sexual, emotional, physical violence, and abuses happened to First Nations children at the hands of people who quoted scripture verses and talked about Jesus. Just a few generations later, the effects of these boundary invasions are evidenced by the alcohol and suicide rates amongst the native people. This abuse, in the name of Jesus, killed the souls of the native people and the scars remain. If you asked these victims if the church is a safe place, they would say, "Absolutely not!" So would others who have experienced hurt and abuse in the name of Yahweh.

We must be wise as serpents and yet gentle as doves when it comes to trusting others in dealing with us, the temple of the Holy Spirit.

Our people, The First Nations people, had many traditions and these were spiritual boundaries to them. When the drum, dance, and regalia were taken from them by the missionaries, they also lost many of their traditions. These traditions were utilized as protective boundaries for the people. As Yahweh is restoring these traditions back to them, the boundaries are being reestablished.

One of those traditions was Protocol. Protocol was our way of saying this is your land or space and I would like to join you in your space. I am humbling myself and offering you a gift and asking to come and join you on your land. May I come join you?

Protocol acknowledged the boundary lines of another. It added a safety net and averted conflict between people. When we lost protocol, we also lost the beauty of seeing one another with boundaries established by Yahweh.

If someone came to native land without practicing protocol it meant war. Protocol was expected and was a way of life for our native people. If Protocol had been practiced in our land, when the immigrants came to America, it might have averted many of the problems and bloodshed that were experienced on our land.

When Suuqiina and I travel in ministry meetings, we have made it a point to practice protocol along the way. Most often, we will not do a seminar in an area without the welcome of the First Nations leaders, the governmental leaders, and the spiritual leaders if the area in which we are teaching.

When we moved to the Tennessee area, we went to Cherokee, North Carolina, and met with the Chief. We brought him a gift. We told him that we knew that the land we were moving to was given to the Cherokee, in stewardship, by the Creator. We shared that, though the land had been taken, that since the gifts and calling of God are irrevocable, that Yahweh had never rescinded stewardship authority from the Cherokee people.

We asked for his blessing to dwell there in peace and prosperity. The Chief welcomed us to the land, released his blessing for peace and prosperity, and said, "I give you authority to speak your message on all land that was originally in the jurisdiction of the Cherokee."

Later that week we went to the Mayor of our city in Tennessee, gifted him, and asked for his blessing to reside in the town. We told him, " We want to let you know that we are moving to your town. We want to be a blessing to you and the city. We know that the Creator has given you authority in this city and we want to honor that. We want to thank you for what you are doing as a leader of this city."

The Mayor was very impressed. No one had ever come to protocol him. He said, " I thought you were here to complain. No one has ever come to present themselves to me like you have. Could you get some more people like you to move in here?"

In his book, *The Gift of Honor,* Gary Smalley says that "honor is a decision we make to place high value, worth and importance on another person by viewing him or her as a priceless gift and granting him or her a position in our lives worthy of great respect. He

> *"We have a tendency to view anyone different from ourselves as less than us."*

also says that the lower the value we attach to a person, the easier we can justify dishonoring them by treating them with disrespect."[8]

This is what happened when the immigrants came to the shores of North America. The Jamestown charter reads that the immigrants came to evangelize savages. That was our first mistake as immigrants. The scriptures say, " I created you in your mother's womb. You are fearfully and wonderfully made (see Psalm 139)." How could they believe that scripture and then view these people as savages? We have a tendency to view anyone different from ourselves as less than us. We devalue them.

A few of our soldiers were able to abuse the prisoners in Iraq because they viewed them as our enemy and as animals. They forgot that the Iraqi's are not viewed that way by Yahweh.

They forgot that they are just as much Yahweh's children as we are. When we devalue a people group, a gender, a denomination, a faith, we will then stoop to behavior that is ungodly and sinful.

When I was a Christian counselor, it troubled me that I had as many adult children of pastors and ministry people as I did adult children of alcoholics and addicts. That did not seem right to me. How could kids who grew up in the church and Christian homes be as messed up as alcoholic's kids. I got the answer, one day, in a group counseling session that I was facilitating. A woman in her late twenties, who was the child of a pastor said this, " You know as a child, it didn't matter to me if my dad was out at church every night or out at a bar every night. All I know is that he wasn't there for me."

She felt worth less than the church. Put the words worth and less together and you get "worthless." Her father honored his commitment to church meetings and the religious hierarchy more than his commitment to his daughter and years later she was feeling the effects.

What broke my heart was that I could reach the children of alcoholics with the message of the love of Yahweh and Yeshua as they were open to a savior. The children of ministry parents were not so easily reached. In their minds it was Yahweh who had taken the time and attention of their parents and so how could He be trusted.

I think it breaks the heart of Yahweh to see His message twisted, perverted, and used to keep people from the intimacy and relationships that He so longs for them to enjoy. It is done, all in His name, through a religious system that He does not endorse or bless.

Mark Dupont says in his book *Walking Out of Spiritual Abuse*, "Spiritual abuse is a horrific crime. It murders the soul and causes trauma in the deepest crevices of the heart. It violently shatters the human spirit, breaking trust at the very core of one's whole being. Accompanying the trauma and hemorrhaging pain, innocence is lost and a sacred trust is betrayed; a trust that may never mend in a world that no longer seems safe."[9]

In the lives of so many "preacher's kids" this is the case. The abuse for them may have come through the lack of boundaries that were never set by their well-meaning parents. Those parents might have believed, as many in church service do, that they were to have no boundaries and that a "good" Christian is there for others, all of the time, day or night. The lack of setting boundaries, in the church, enables abuse and neglect of children to flourish.

If we truly honor others, we must think before we invade their personal land. The law of respect or honor in Matthew 7:12 says, "In everything, therefore, treat people the same way you would want them to treat you, for this is the Law of the Prophets."

In order to do this, we must also get out of our own thinking and selves enough to observe them and ask these questions. How are they different from me? If their culture is different from mine how do they experience honor in their culture? How do they experience love? It might be very different from how we would experience love and honor.

Warfare by Honor

In his book, *The Five Love Languages*, Gary Chapman writes, "we must be willing to learn the love languages of others if we are to be effective communicators of love."[10]

We, as believers in Yeshua, have been given the ministry of reconciliation. Isn't that remarkable? Yahweh has entrusted us with the greatest message of all time, the gospel message. And yet, so often, we don't even take the time to learn about the people that he has sent us to and what moves their hearts.

Our country pays big bucks to Ambassadors who represent our country before the nations. Other countries send their ambassadors here to build relationships between their country and ours. These ambassadors are well versed in the protocols of each country so as not to offend the people with whom they are partnering.

Corporate America also knows the power of protocol and trains their employees well in the art of global etiquette. In fact, if you go 'online' and enter the word 'protocol' in a web search, you will be amazed at how many protocol schools come before your very eyes. It seems the corporate world understands the scripture that says, "It is easier to win a whole city than a brother who is offended."

Our military also uses protocol. In fact the medical field, the law, the field of education, and the field of computers all utilize protocol. How can it be then, that as ambassadors of the King of the greatest kingdom of all eternity, we as believers in Yeshua have failed to practice honor through protocol? It doesn't make sense and it is time for us to reclaim this honorable tool of restoration. Honorable protocol will open doors that no man can shut and will release the miraculous in ways our finite minds can not understand.

When I first began to be restored to the practice of proto-col in my own life, it felt awkward and I felt like a child learning to walk for the first time. It was humbling to have to ask for author-ity to be released to me when I had been taught to "take" authority in the name of Jesus. One day when I was struggling, Yeshua spoke to my heart and this is what He said, "Qaumaniq, I own the land that you set your feet on and I own you. You are the steward, right?" I said, "Yes, Lord, I am the steward and you own everything including me." He said,

"How can we do any less than to respect one another the way He has showed us by example?"

&

"I own everything, including you, and yet my protocol concern-ing the people I have created is this, "Behold I stand at the door and knock, if anyone hears my voice and opens the door, I will come in a dine with him and he with Me (see Rev. 3:20)." He continued, "Qaumaniq, if anyone bashes your door down, it is not Me, it is a religious spirit. And if you bash anyone else's door down, it is not Me, it is a religious spirit. I protocol my people with the gift of life and the gift of choice. Though I am the Creator of the universe, I am a man of honor and will not bash the boundaries of my people."

How can we do any less than to respect one another the way He has shown us by example? How can we allow others to defile us, made of dirt from His own hands, the land that he owns and respects? We can not do any less than be people of honor who reflect his character through us.

Warfare by Honor

We can be people that rebuild the ancient ruins but we will

not be able to do it without honor. Protocol is the vehicle that

releases the honor that is formed and fashioned in our hearts.

Chapter Three

Examples of Protocol From the Scriptures

Now that you are learning about protocol, you will be able to identify areas in your life where you have been operating with protocol but were unaware of it. Several years ago I purchased a canary yellow Honda. I thought it was a one-of-a-kind automobile since I had never seen another one like it. An interesting thing began to happen, I began to notice canary yellow Hondas everywhere I went. They were always present but I was not aware of them until I had my own. This is the same phenomenon you may experience concerning protocol.

The scriptures are full of protocol. You have probably read the following accounts many times but this time we'll read them as stories that include aspects of protocol.

Creative Protocol

From the beginning the Scriptures reveal patterns of protocol. The creation account, beginning in Genesis, clearly reveals a creative protocol that was neither accidental nor was it incidental. It was definitely inspired, profound and divine in origin.

The creative protocol begins with an irrefutable announcement that "Elohim created the heavens and the earth." This announcement protocol is upheld throughout the scriptures as Elohim announces Himself as "the Elohim of Abraham,

"...protocol doesn't just happen, it is planned and announced."

Isaac, and Jacob." This announcement protocol is used in the introduction of Yeshua as the Messiah by the angel Gabriel to Mary. Many indigenous tribes begin their protocol with the announcement of their name, lineage, and heritage. I think the Creator set an example for mankind in the first of His revelations to man. Remember, protocol doesn't just happen, it is planned and announced.

The second protocol is the separation between light and darkness. It set forth an ability to discern things both in the natural and supernatural. This ability led to an understanding of our experience of "day" and "night." It cannot be overlooked that the biblical protocol of what we refer to as a "day' actually begins in the "evening." The Hebrews later began to reference this with an exact time, six o'clock p.m. This "daytime" experience was practiced throughout history until the times and seasons were changed (without Sovereign authority) and the daytime began to be observed beginning at midnight. The Jews continue to honor this biblical daytime protocol and begin their day at six p.m. (some Jews begin their day

at the actual sundown) If we had continued the biblical understanding of "day" and "night," our watches would have the "6"
at the top instead of the "12."

The third protocol was the division of dirt and water. This
would prove to be quite important when the time came for the
creation of land animals and sea animals. It might be interesting to note here that the Hebrew root of the name Elohim
means justice. In the reading of the scriptures where Elohim
surveys His creation and says that "it was good," is actually ren-
dered in the Hebrew as "it was right (correct)." Justice saw what
He created and declared them to be "right" for their purposes.
Land is "right" for cows and oceans are "right" for whales, etc.

On the third day Elohim created grass, plants, trees, and
seeds of them for perpetuating the creation. He saw that "it
was right."

On the fourth day He created signs, appointed times, days
and years through specific light separations called the sun,
moon, and stars. He saw "this was right."

On the fifth day he created sea creatures to swim and birds
to fly above the dirt and there He blessed His creation with a
prophetic proclamation to multiply in the earth (see Gen
1:22). Again, He saw that "it was right."

He also called forth in creation the livestock, creeping creatures and the beasts of the field. He saw they were "right."

On the sixth day the creation protocol changes dramati-
cally. Here Elohim recreates government by creating man
(generic at this point containing both the male and female
likeness of Elohim –see Gen.1:27) to be an earth steward, or
ruler over all the previous creation elements. He imparts a
prophetic blessing over them to increase and fill the earth and

to partake of the creation for food, at this time limiting food to the green plants of the earth. Elohim's survey of His creation and the inclusion of mankind is given a heightened summary as He states "it is very (completely) right."

Again on the seventh day, Elohim reveals creative protocol. The scriptures (see Gen.2:2) say that the creative work was "completed" by the blessing and "setting apart" of the seventh day as a day of rest. This rest does not imply that Elohim was exhausted from His creating. It is revealing His absolute Sovereignty to choose something, in this case a certain day, as a personal possession amongst all that He had created. The scriptures never reveal any authority given to anyone to alter and change this sovereign choice. In fact the opposite is revealed (see Daniel 7:25), that man *takes authority to himself* to change both the "appointed times and the Torah." The Sabbath is an appointed time by Elohim revealing His headship over all creation. The Israelites were commanded to keep the Sabbath **before** the giving of the Torah at Sinai (see Exodus 16:23-30). The religious system, labeled the New Roman Religion, overthrew Yahweh's sovereign decree in 325 A.D. at the Council of Nicea, and chose the new "Sol dei," "day of the sun" as a day set apart for worship and religion. At the Council of Laodicea, this new Sunday became law with enforcement of the death penalty for anyone "honoring and keeping" the Sabbath. The prophet Isaiah (see Is.66:23) assures us the Sabbath will again be the faith and practice of all believers when Yahweh sets up His Kingdom on earth. This seventh day protocol cannot be ignored without the peril of discounting the Sovereignty of Elohim.

The protocol of creation is a powerful revelation of Elohim's relationship with His creation. It is not only a "right" protocol, it is an exact one with truths and implications that reach into eternity. The understanding of creative protocol may not be fully known until He comes to "recreate the heavens and the earth." The power and wonder of this creative protocol encourages us to agree with the psalmist (Ps.8:4-6,1) "What is man that You remember him? And the son of man that You visit him? Yet You have made him a little lower than Elohim, And have crowned him with esteem and splendor. You made him rule over the works of Your hands; You have put all under his feet, O Yahweh, our Master, how excellent is Your Name in all the earth."

> *"The protocol of creation is a powerful revelation of Elohim's relationship with His creation."*

The Order (Protocol) of Melchizedek

The full account of Melchizedek can be read in Genesis 14, Psalm 110, and in Hebrews 5-8. Here is a brief look at the protocol in the Genesis account.

The story is about the rescuing of Abraham's brother, Lot. After a military victory, Abraham passes through the city-state ruled by a King, Prophet, and Priest named Melchizedek. Notice the protocol that takes place here.

Three important characters are mentioned here, Abraham, Melchizedek, and the King of Sodom. These three meet in the Sovereign's Valley and we can see that Melchizedek places himself between Abraham and the King of Sodom. Here is the first biblical account of a human intercessor, someone that stands between the profitable intention on one side and the destructive intentions on the other.

Melkchizedek was a priest of El Elyon, a name that Abraham does not know. Abraham does not attempt to replace this Divine relationship with his own relationship nor does he refuse the revelation of El Elyon as the "Possessor of the heavens and the earth." Abraham, in fact, adds that revelatory name to his own prayer saying, "I have lifted my hand to Yahweh, the El Elyon, the Possessor of the heavens and the earth...etc."

It might be noted that many indigenous people have a revelatory name and relationship with Yahweh. Many times missionaries, in their mono-cultural paradigm of the gospel, have discounted or even thought demonic any indigenous reference to the Creator. Abraham, as a man of protocol and promise, is insightfully receptive to this Melchizedek. His spirit bears witness with this indigenous ruler.

Melchizedek gives Abraham bread and wine in protocol. The honoring in multi-cultural relationships begins with nourishment and comfort, not humiliation and arrogance. This protocol is prophetic as these nourishment's point to the protocol of the communion of the biblical "called out ones". Many times the focus has been upon the elements themselves, the bread and wine, and not on the significance of the protocol that is happening before our very eyes. The bread and wine also commemorate the wedding of man and woman as Adam prophecies (see Gen.2:23).."This is now bone of my bones and flesh of my flesh..." The bone marrow produces the blood and the flesh signifies the bread and thus the communion becomes the most significant act of intimacy between the bride and bridegroom.

Then Melchizedek pronounces a blessing, a welcome if you will, over Abraham. He acknowledges Abraham as being "of" El

Elyon. He acknowledges the victory Abraham has received by El Elyon. He not only honors Abraham, he receives and includes Abraham into his own relationship with El Elyon. Here is the greater, Melchizedek, blessing the lesser, Abraham (see Hebrews 5-8). The proper welcoming protocol is to share and not withhold the blessing from a guest or stranger. Melchizedek speaks the blessing so Abraham will have something to hold onto after leaving Salem. Melchizedek affirms Abraham and recognizes his accomplishments. He lifts Abraham up, he intercedes for him in the presence of the King of Sodom who is there to steal Abraham's honor.

> *"The proper welcoming protocol is to share and not withhold the blessing from a guest or stranger."*

Abraham, in proper protocol, gifts Melchizedek with a tenth of the spoils of war. Here the immigrant gives to the indigenous ruler. Many times the immigrants have stolen from the indigenous peoples of the world. The proper protocol is set forth in Abraham as we are considered, by faith, to be his "seed." This mutual gifting is restated in Corinthians about spiritual gifts being "gifts for the whole Body." It would have been easily understood if Abraham had considered the spoils of his victory as hard won or even reimbursement for the tremendous investment in the rescue of his brother. Abraham's life message is not about accumulating wealth but about receiving a promise.

Abraham does not steal any of Melchizedek's honor nor does he belittle the protocol of this King. Abraham understands government. He recognizes authority and makes no attempt to usurp it or diminish its power. He is not a "robber and a thief" that Yeshua mentions in John's gospel chapter ten. He stays at the gate and lets the gatekeeper impart authority to him. Have you noticed that people with genuine authority never have to tell anyone they have it? If anyone lacks the authority to accomplish any assignment, there is a proper way to obtain it and usurping it is not it. This is a powerful protocol lesson. It is so powerful that Yeshua declares that His relationship with Yahweh is not like the protocol of the Levites, but it is the protocol of Melchizedek (see Hebrews 5-8).

Over and over again, in John's gospel, Yeshua states that he does not speak His own words but speaks only what He hears from Yahweh. He says He does not do anything but what He sees Abba doing. He declares that His authority comes from "above" and is not something He has stolen or usurped. He also states that His followers are people like Himself, people of protocol. His last words to the called out ones is "he that has ears let him hear what the Spirit is saying." This is what it means to "be like Yeshua." This is what it means to be "conformed to His image (see Romans 8)." The true followers of Yeshua are people of honor, people of protocol. It has become their character. They are people who recognize true authority and any authority that may become necessary for divine purposes is sought after in honorable ways.

I believe this protocol between Melchizedek and Abraham was the foundation for Abraham's strength to refute the temptation to share, with the King of Sodom, the spoils of his victory. One is reminded of the account of Gehazi, Elisha's servant, and his decision to share in the material wealth of Naaman. His reward was leprosy, a disease that literally eats up the material, man's flesh. Abraham had sworn an oath to not share the spoils lest he would face the charge of being made "rich" outside the providence of El Elyon. With Melchizedek's honorable protocol, the refreshment and nourishment, the fellowship, the insight and revelation, the imparting of authority, and the exchange of gifts, Abraham is well able to fulfill his vow and withstand King Bera's temptations.

The nourishing, comforting, and blessing to Abraham in protocol called forth in Abraham the character of El Elyon, the true Possessor of heaven and earth. In the indigenous cultures, wealth is not determined by what one can accumulate but rather by what is extravagantly given away. It is no wonder that the Euro-Americans did not appreciate and even outlawed the native potlatch because it was so opposite of their definition of wealth which is, "accumulation without end."

The protocol does not end in Genesis fourteen. This protocol leads to the prophetic vision Yahweh has for Abraham and his seed (see Gen. 15). Proper protocol is not the road to success, it is the *gate* that opens to that road. It is a gate that shouldn't be ignored.

Yaweh visits Abraham—Genesis 18

Here is an account of Mid-Eastern protocol of hospitality. It is, however, a pattern that seems to be followed by indigenous people everywhere albeit with differing details.

The scriptures tell us Adonai and two angels are traveling through Abraham's land. Abraham implores them not to pass by his tent but to be given an opportunity to show his hospitality. His protocol begins with a sincere and urgent welcome.

He immediately calls for water, both for refreshment and to wash their dusty, dirty feet. He instructs them to rest under a shade tree and informs them that he will nourish them with bread. He probably remembered the nourishing he received in the valley with Melchizedek. They receive his welcome and follow his instructions.

These heavenly dignitaries understand protocol because heaven is place where the atmosphere is one of protocol and honor. You can read in the book of Revelation the elaborate protocol ceremonies that appear in heaven. When we pray the prayer Yeshua taught us we say, "let Your will be done on earth as it is in heaven…" What we are saying is that protocol and honor is to be manifested on earth in the same manner as it is in heaven. Elohim established the protocols that are to occur on earth. One can read in the book of Hebrews the protocol of the High Priest and how man can come to Yahweh. These three heavenly visitors to Abraham and Sarah knew what would be expected of them but they let Abraham reveal his own heart of hospitality to them. The scriptures tell us that we have "entertained angels without knowing it." Maybe we have been visited by heavenly dignitaries in order to have our hearts revealed.

Sarah begins making fresh bread for them. Everyone loves the nourishment of fresh bread and nothing compares with the aroma of bread as it is baked. Yeshua tells us He is the "bread of life" and we can be nourished by His presence in us. That special aroma of fresh bread ought to be what followers of Yeshua smell like.

In the meanwhile, Abraham goes and picks out his best calf to be prepared for his guests. Think of the generous heart displayed here. Abraham gives a significant portion of his wealth, a portion of his future, part of the increase of his herd, and something of great personal value to his family as a sacrifice for these guests. What a great example of a person of selfless integrity and generosity this is.

In verse eight the scriptures tell us that Abraham set this beautiful meal before them and then "stood by them" as a waiter would stand near in a fine restaurant. He is not only their host but also their servant. He does exactly what Melchizedek had done for him. He blesses them, he serves them, and he waits on them. His strength of character and the power of his authority shine forth in this protocol of hospitality.

Then the heavenly guests bless Abraham and Sarah with a prophetic promise concerning their future inheritance by the birth of a son to them. One can imagine how this blessing must have encouraged Abraham's heart since he had already received the prophetic promises given in chapter twelve of becoming a great nation and a global family. His protocol of hospitality is well rewarded but he didn't do it for the reward, he did it because it was right, it was proper protocol.

The reward became even greater as Adonai decided to protocol Abraham by sharing with him what His plans were for Sodom and Gomorrah (see Genesis 18:16-33). One of Adonai's protocols is to share part of the future with trusted followers and friends of the Kingdom. In one prophetic book it says He "does nothing without first telling His prophets." It is part of His hospitality as Owner of the earth. Humans are Elohim's guests on this planet, He is the host. Part of having a personal relationship with Yahweh involves the intimacy of knowing what some of His plans are and working, together with Him, for the fulfillment of those plans. His protocol is to share His will and purpose with us as His guests on earth.

This account of hospitality is repeated in the scriptures. You can read the account of a father and his two sons, one of which becomes a prodigal. Upon his return, the father sets forth a banquet quite similar to Abraham's. All attempts at proper hospitality ought to be accompanied by proper protocol.

The examples of protocol that could be taken from the scriptures are too many to even list in this handbook. A short list would include clothing; the clothing of men and women, the talit, tse tse, the kippa, the headband, etc., food and meals, education, the family, social and political groups, government, warfare, religion, and spiritual activities.

"The scriptures reveal the protocols of life as given through a 'father's instructions to his children' (torah)."

Many of the scriptural protocols are quite elaborate such as the temple worship protocol. Worship of Yahweh that is in "spirit and in truth" is not an informal, haphazard affair. It involves ceremony, pageantry, order, and protocol. Some of the protocols were equally informal such as the naming ceremony or the circumcision ceremony. These were straightforward, simple protocols but filled with great meaning for everyone involved with them.

The scriptures reveal the protocols of life as given through a "father's instructions to his children" (torah). This life was expected to be full and fulfilling, abundant, free, joyful, loving, truthful, peaceful, kind, gracious, hospitable, visionary, creative, obedient, fun, serious, caring, emotional, rational, spiritual, and most of all, real. Yahweh is not a giant 'kill joy,' holding His thumb over us, ready to smash us when we make an error. He is for us! He also knows that some part of our beings love to please Him, so He provided the means to do just that. Scriptural protocols help us fulfill our desire to please our Creator.

When we examine the lives of the patriarchs, we see people who understood the power of protocol.

Jacob and Esau

It was a very serious matter when Jacob tricked his father, Isaac, into gifting him with the first and largest blessing (see Gen.27). The proper protocol was for the first born son to receive the double portion blessing and his father's inheritance. Isaac knew that once he released the blessing he could not rescind it. Jacob went against that protocol knowing that Esau would likely be offended and may even seek revenge. Jacob left his home and moved far away so he wouldn't have to contend with his brother's wrath.

Later, when Jacob was led by Yahweh to return to the land of his father, he had to deal with the unfinished business with his brother, Esau. It says (see Gen. 32) that "his gifts went out before him." Jacob knew the power of protocol. "And he spent the night there, and took what came to his hand as a gift for Esau his brother—two hundred female goats, twenty male goats, two hundred ewes, twenty rams, thirty milk camels with their colts, forty cows, ten bulls, twenty female donkeys, and forty foals. And he gave into the hands of his servants, every drove by itself, and said to his servants, "Pass over before me, and put some distance between drove and drove." And he commanded the first one saying, "When Esau, my brother, meets you and asks saying, "To whom do you belong, and where are you going? And whose are these in front of you? Then you shall say, "They are your servant Jacob's. It is a gift sent to my master, Esau. And see, he is also behind us." So Jacob commanded the second, and the third, and all who followed the droves saying, "Speak to Esau this same word when you find him. And you shall say, "Also look, your servant Jacob is behind us." For he said, "Let me appease him with the gift that goes before me, and after that I shall see his face. He might accept me. And his gifts went out ahead of him."

Jacob humbled himself and practiced protocol. Genuine and correct protocol is always accompanied by humility.

The Ten Commandments

In Exodus 20, Yahweh issues His protocol in a document called the Torah. The Ten Commandments are attitudes and actions that Yahweh expects people, who are called by His name, to acknowledge and implement in their lives. They are part of a father's instruction to his children (Torah). Later on Yahweh gives the consequences of those who disobey Him.

The Magi

In Matthew 2 is the account of the birth of Yeshua.

And having been born in Bethlehem of Judah in the days of Herod the king, see Magi from the East came to Jerusalem, saying, "Where is he who has been born King of the Jews? For we saw his star in the East and have come to do rever - ence (protocol) to him.

And coming into the house, they saw the child with Miryam, His mother, and fell down and did reverence to him, and opening their treasures, they presented to him gifts of gold, frankincense, and myrh. (see Matt. 2:1; 2:11)

This well-known story of the "three wise men" is a perfect picture of protocol. Knowing the signs written in the stars, they came with protocol gifts worthy of a king.

Ruth and Naomi

In the book of Ruth we are told the story of Naomi, her family, Ruth, Orpah, Boaz, and the covenant relationship they unfold.

Naomi, a Hebrew, moves to Moab with her husband and two sons, due to a famine in Israel. The two sons marry Moabite women. Then the husband and both sons die leaving Naomi, Ruth, and Orpah as widows. Naomi determines to return to Israel, to her clan. She encourages her daughter-in-laws to remain in Moab and remarry there. She, undoubtedly, is attempting to spare them the difficulties associated with cross-cultural and inter-racial relationships.

And Naomi said to her two daughters-in-law, "Go, return each to her mother's house, Yahweh show kindness to you, as you have shown to the dead and me. Yahweh grant that you find rest, each in the house of her husband." Then she kissed them and they lifted up their voices and wept. And they said to her, "No, we shall go back with you to your peo - ple." But Naomi said, "Go back my daughters, why go with me?" (Ruth 1:8)

And they lifted up their voices and wept again. And Orpah kissed her mother-in-law, but Ruth clung to her. And she said, "Look your sister-in-law has gone back to her people

and to her mighty ones. Go back, follow your sister-in-law."
But Ruth said, Do not urge me to leave you, or to go back
from following after you. For wherever you go, I go: and
wherever you stop, I stop. Your people are my people and
your Elohim is my Elohim. Where you die I die, and there I
shall be buried. Yahweh do so to me, and more also—for
death itself parts you and me (Ruth 1:14).

These verses are used in many marriage ceremonies to convey the depth of covenant relationship between marriage partners. However, rarely have we been taught the prophetic significance that is within the story or the teaching of protocol that Ruth used in her dealing with Naomi.

Ruth loved her mother-in-law but she was also responding as a righteous woman, a woman of integrity that had the Torah written on her heart. Although she was gentile by birth, she followed the Hebrew protocol in her dealings with Naomi. The story also teaches us the protocol of caring for widows.

And the Levite, because he has no portion of your inheri-
tance with you, and the sojourner and the fatherless, and
the widow who are within your gates, shall come and eat
and be satisfied, so that Yahweh your Elohim does bless you
in all the work of your hand which you do (Deut. 14:29).

When you reap your harvest in your field, and have forgotten
a sheaf in the field, do not go back to get it. Let it be for the
stranger, for the fatherless, and for the widow (Deut.24:18).

Clean and undefiled religion before Elohim and Father is this:
to take care of orphans and widows in their affliction and to
keep ones self unstained from the world (James 1:27).

How many churches or professing believers have financial, relational, and emotional support, for widows and orphans, as line items in their budgets? The word of Yahweh states, clearly, that such support is what defines pure and undefiled religion. Are we following His protocol concerning widows and orphans? We have found that a majority of believers are unaware or simply unconcerned with this protocol.

The Ruth passage has another equally important message of protocol that we address in the chapter on Israel.

Personal gifts

Yahweh has given protocol gifts to everyone. Dreams, desires, callings, ministries, talents, opportunities, and responsibilities are all gifts from the Creator.

And there are different kinds of gifts, but the same Spirit. There are different kinds of services but the same Master. And there are different kinds of workings, but it is the same Elohim who is working in all. And to each one is given the manifestation of the Spirit for profiting (1 Cor. 12:4-7).

It says "the gifts and callings of Yahweh are irrefutable (see Rom.11:29)." Once a gift has been given it cannot be taken back. They are given "for keeps."

A man's gifts make room for him and brings him before great men (Prov.18:16).

Always remember, we are spiritual beings having a human experience, not the other way around. Our experience of humanness is quite short but our spiritual existence will go on forever. The scriptural protocols help us live our human experience and at the same time prepare us for our forever experience. The protocols redirect our behaviors and philosophy of life so our characters can be shaped with the values of eternity. These scriptural protocols should not be overlooked or ignored. They were given with our best interests in mind.

Some of the scriptural protocols seem very foreign to us Westerners and they are. We aren't expected to replicate them into our culture but we are expected to see the values they contain and replicate those into our own lives. Sometimes examining someone else's culture helps us remember our own culture and what may have been set aside. There are good, powerful, and positive elements of everyone's cultures that need to be restored. The scriptural protocols can help us regain those things that have been lost.

When you read the scriptures, ask yourself if some practice of protocol is included in the passage you are reading. Ask yourself what values are being expressed by that protocol. Then ask yourself if those values are resident in your own life. You'll be surprised how full the scriptures are with protocol and how they will "come to life" for you as you examine them.

Chapter Four

Honoring the Elders

"Being unwanted, unloved, uncared for,
forgotten by everybody,
I think that is a much greater hunger,
a much greater poverty than the person
who has nothing to eat, we must find each other."
Mother Teresa—Catholic Missionary
Cited in *More of ...The Best of Bits and Pieces*

In the 1970's The Chrysler Corporation was on the verge of going under. The company was losing millions of dollar's everyday. The company hired Lee Iacocca to be the CEO to try to save the company. Lee had worked for Ford for 32 years and had been President of Ford for eight years. It took Lee a few years, but he was successful in turning the company around and made Chrysler a profitable company once again.

What was the secret to Lee's success? In addition to his own personal experience and ability, he relied on retired executives from Ford, who had been his colleagues. These individuals came out of retirement to aid Lee and the Chrysler Corporation. They were instrumental in turning this company around.

Lee Iacocca made a wise choice when he gathered his team to tackle this challenging task. He knew the value of the wisdom of the elders. These former employees of Ford, who had stepped down from their careers in the corporate world due to their age, possessed within them a wealth of information and were a priceless source of wisdom to Mr. Iacocca. Utilizing these retired individuals was the silver bullet for Chrysler.

In his book, Lee Iococca said that the elderly could help the younger generation from making many unnecessary mistakes that could be destructive to them. "The Oriental Mind says, the longer you live, the smarter you get. There's not just respect, there's reverence. Many of the people who run Japan are in there eighties. They've lived long enough and gotten wise enough, at least, to protect their young people from self-destruction. Nothing is new to them; they've seen it come and go."[1]

We recently read a great book about finances called *Rich Dad Poor Dad* written by Robert T. Kiyosaki.[2] This book is the #1 New York Times Bestseller. The book was an eye opener for us in the area of finances. The book tells about what rich dads teach their children about money that the middle class and poor dads do not. The book is basically a financial book that passes on the wisdom of the previous generation to the next generation. Throughout the book, Robert quotes his

"Rich Dad" many times and the wisdom that was passed down to him by this man. Robert shares his story of how he has followed his "Rich Dad's" wisdom and shows how this wisdom, put into practice, has made him a rich and wise man himself. Hundreds of thousands of people are buying this book. The book is not magical, it is simply a book of elderly wisdom.

Robert is of Japanese decent. He comes from a culture that honors the elders. His honoring of the elders most likely helped Robert to see the value in this mentor and enabled him to humble himself to receive from this man.

"In American society, elders, many times, are seen as a burden and caring for them is not a gift but a drudgery."

In American society, elders, many times, are seen as a burden and caring for them is not a gift but a drudgery. Elders are not looked to for the wisdom that is locked within their mind and hearts but instead are treated as a left over meal that is pushed to the back of the refrigerator and forgotten only to be thrown away at a later date.

Sadly, because honoring of the elders has been lost in our society, we don't even realize that some day, if we are fortunate to live long enough, we too will be elders. If we truly believed the scriptures and what they say regarding the process of sowing and reaping (see Gal. 6:7), we would be very concerned considering that we, as a society, are sowing dishonor and neglect in unfathomable proportions.

"By the year 2020, 1.1 billion people are expected to be over the age of 65."[3] This will be challenging at best. In our country, as the baby boomer generation reaches retirement age, we are being warned that Social Security cannot and will not be able to support the burgeoning requirements that will be needed to sustain that generation. Because we have not mentored our children well in the art of honoring the elders, the boomer generation is now facing a problem it has created. The baby boomers will now need the support and honor from a generation that has been neglected and is not prepared for such a task.

"Elders are people who have weathered many of life's storms and are wiser for it."

Elders are not just people who are chronologically older than we are. Elders are people who have weathered many of life's storms and are wiser for it. Because they have lived and learned, they have the ability to see the whole picture in situations. They can see from many perspectives. This gives them the ability to discern options to problems of which younger, less experienced people might not be aware.

By the time one reaches the time of being an elder, they most often have made it through one or more serious challenges or tragedies in life. The fact that they are still here and intact offers comfort to younger people that they too will survive and may even prosper, despite the most horrific of circumstances life can deal to mankind.

"Middle-aged people need the elderly, although they may not know it or even believe it, " says one 78-year-old woman, "To grow older themselves, younger people need the lessons that can be learned only from caring for their parents." I (Qaumaniq) know that this is true because I learned a lot from my own grandparents. Whenever our family would be in cri-sis, my grandparents would come and stay for a visit to help out with what was needed. What they provided for me, as a child, was a sense of security and stability.

When I was in my thirties, I got a serious illness that caused me to be bedridden a good deal of the time. I was unable to drive or do any of my regular household activities. Needless to say, my life drastically slowed down. At thirty, I got to see what it felt like to be an elderly person as far as lim-itations and helplessness was concerned. I found, during that time, that I connected better to the elderly than to people my own age. I also got to feel the emotions the elderly feel of being left behind.

I had to give up my home and car and move in with others that could help take care of me. This was very humbling and I was sad as I said goodbye to my freedom and much of the dig-nity that I felt as a self-supporting person. It was a time of great grief in my life as I went through all my belongings to downsize. Since I was moving in with others, I would not have room for the things I had collected along the way.

I remember feeling so much like a burden when the fami-ly that I moved in with had to move things around to make room for me. I also felt bad when they had to shuffle their schedules to drive me to doctors' appointments or to run an errand for me. The shame, at times, was overwhelming and I felt like it might have been better if I just did not exist. I real-ized, then, that most people would face this same experience, if they lived long enough to reach their twilight years.

One incredible blessing, though, was being able to spend time with the children in this family, which became grandchildren to me. Because I was restrained, due to the illness, I was available to spend time with them and become a support in their lives. They came to rely on me for hugs, advice and security and I came to rely on them for a reason to continue to live. This next generation needed me around therefore I could not give up on life. What remains today is a solid, loving relationship with these children, who still see I am another person in their lives who will be there, should they need me. I am also a person that will make an effort to love and support them regardless of how they perform.

I have long since healed and moved from the home of my grandchildren and am now involved in traveling and speaking in venues all over the country. I have to say that as I look back, I believe that the most important and rewarding time of my life, outside of parenting my own children, was the time that I served in the capacity of an elder in the lives of these children.

Recently I was looking through some papers and came upon this letter from my granddaughter. In it she expresses the heart of what an elder brings to the life of a child.

Dear Nana,

When I first found out you were moving I was mad! Because it felt like you came into our lives sick and ready to die, but we wouldn't let you go. You pulled through and in the process we fell in love with you. We adopted you into our family.

Then you got busy and I really missed being able to talk to you late at night, and hug and kiss you before I went to bed. Now you are moving as far away as anyone can, and still be in the same country! (Alaska) I understand though, that it's

God's will for you to move, and that is the only thing that keeps me from crying myself to sleep each night.

I will miss you horribly, and will wait impatiently for the time when I can come to visit you in your beautiful paradise. The hardest thing will be not being able to hug and kiss you goodnight, the absence of your understanding and caring heart, your UNFAILING input, your wonderful laugh, and the way you looked whenever you dyed your hair!

You stuck with us through happy and sad times, good and bad. We've been through hell more than once, and together we survived. I just wanted to say thanks and I love you and always will.

Luv-U-4-Ever,

This shows the bond that can happen between the elders and the young if we will take time enough to permit it to happen. These children, my grandchildren, willed me to live by placing a demand on the gifts and wisdom that Yahweh had placed inside of me. Because of them I had a purpose and was no longer a throwaway.

So it can be for all our elders if we will take the time to honor and invest in them.

We are missing some of the greatest gifts life has to offer. Most people, like most wine, get better with age.

King Solomon said in his writings "there is nothing new under the sun." This is true of life's problems. There are many challenges in life, some with a   personalized twist added. For example, most traumatic events that we will encounter in life as humans, involve financial challenges, health problems of our own or a loved one, problems in child rearing, rela-tional difficulties in the home or job, and dealing with our death or the death of a loved one. There are others, but these are common to all. However, rarely does the average American take the time to consult an elder person on any of these matters, although the eld-ers have been through more than one of these challenges and have come out on the other side of them. It doesn't sound very wise does it? It is as if we would rather figure everything out for ourselves and make our own tragic mistakes than learn from someone else. It is either very foolish or pridefully arrogant.

"Anyone that claims to be spiritual and does not honor their elders is fooling themselves!"

When I was ill, the person who gave me the most comfort and encouragement was a woman named Dot Hathcock. In her seventies, she was forty years my senior, but was an incredible woman with whom to spend time. She was never too busy to take my calls and encourage me that I could sur-vive the trials I was going through. She shared the times she had encountered similar trials and lived to teach about them.

During a tragic and scary time in my life, she added wis-dom, instruction, spiritual mentoring and security. Without her support I might not have made it through.

I recently came upon a scripture in the book of Ruth. Ruth was devoted to her mother-in-law, Naomi, after the death of Naomi's husband and the death of her own husband, Naomi's son. Ruth was so faithful to honor her elder that she was rewarded, by receiving Boaz, as her kinsman redeemer. The scripture says that Ruth found favor in the eyes of Boaz and she said, "Why have I found favor in your eyes, that you should take notice of me, seeing I am a foreigner?" And Boaz answered and said to her, "I have been told all that you have done for your mother-in-law since the death of your husband, and how you have left your father and your mother and the land of your birth, and have come to a people whom you did not know before. Yahweh repay your work, and your reward is complete from Yahweh Elohim of Israel, under whose wings you have come to seek refuge (see Ruth 2:10-12)." Yahweh, Himself, will honor and reward those who honor their elders. Anyone that claims to be spiritual and does not honor their elders is fooling themselves!

Many of the religions of the world practice honor of the elderly in some way. The Scriptures say that elders are worthy of honor and esteem. They are designed by Yahweh (see Titus 1:5).

In 1Timothy 5:17 the Apostle Paul says, "Let the elders who rule well be counted worthy of double honor, especially those who labor in the word and doctrine."

This shows that it was a given that the elders would be honored. To those who ruled well, double honor was bestowed. The elders were expected to make decisions for the entire community. They were expected to be leaders in every sense of the word, not in position and name only. They were to admonish and gently rebuke others who needed correction, and they were to be responsible for the other people in the community. This does not mean that they were to be overly authoritative or bossy but to be available and involved in the lives of those to whom they were responsible.

Warfare by Honor

In the Jewish culture, it is not only rude to interrupt an elder, it is prohibited by Jewish law. When the Apostle Paul wrote "let the women learn in silence," he was not being misogynistic but, rather, applying the learning practice that was already in place for the male students. Besides not interrupting him/her, it is forbidden to sit or stand in his/her place or to contradict him/her. It is also required that one rise to honor the elder when an elder enters the room.

There is a story told by the sage Abba Ha-kohen bar Papa. "When he would be walking on the road and see people ahead of him he would take another road so that the people would not be troubled to rise in his presence. Another sage, Rabi Yosei criticized the behavior of Abba Ha-kohen. Rabi Yosei said that Rabbi Ha-kohen should have passed in front of those people and given them the opportunity to rise in his presence and in so doing express their awe for Yahweh."[4] This act of honoring an elder is akin to honoring Yahweh. This practice can and should be restored in our own culture.

Moses petitioned Yahweh that the burden of carrying the leadership of all the people was too much for him (see Numbers 11:11-14). Yahweh responded by instructing Moses to gather seventy elders to help him with the burden. These elders would help Moses lead the people and their wisdom would be utilized to govern righteously. The honoring of elders actually promotes democracy. The fact that Moses shared his authority with the elders provided protection against his forming a dictatorship.

Yahweh instructed the priests, who were the Levites, that those age twenty-five and upward would do the work in the service of the tent of meeting. From age fifty they should withdraw from the work of service in the tent of meeting and serve no more. Instead, they would then begin to minister to their brethren in the tent of meeting, to keep their charge. At age fifty they moved from a position of doing work in the tent of meeting to a position of elder where they would be utilized in the areas of leadership and wisdom.

To revere someone as an elder is the highest tribute that can be paid to an individual. In the indigenous cultures of the world, this is common. The elders, in many indigenous societies, are the ones who govern the tribe. They are seen as the wisest of the wise. Native children are taught, from the time they are young, that the elders are due honor. One of the most dishonorable things a native can do is to dishonor an elder. In the Inuit culture a young adult will not speak to an elder until the elder addresses them first.

In most native tribal meetings, the elders are given the seats of honor in the center of the circle. Unlike contemporary non-native societies, elders are sought after for their wisdom and advice. It is seen as an honor to take care of the elders and they are never seen as a burden.

All tribal people are preparing for the day when they will become elders of their tribe. This will be a season in life in which they will need to have wisdom and discernment in order to lead the whole tribe in decisions. The way they prepare is not the conventional way, by asking questions and learning through books. Instead, the native people learn through observation and listening.

As children, being trained to hunt or fish, they were instructed that their first catch or kill was to be given to an elder. Children are taught from a young age to always take care of the elders. They are instructed to make sure that the elders have food, that they are warm in the winter, and that they have the medicines they need. The children are taught to give up their seats for the elders and to see that the elders are cared for in a good way. It is the children's responsibility, in the tribe, to serve the elders. This teaches the children about respect. It is common at potlatches and native gatherings, when food is served, for the elders to be served first, even before the children.

In the fall of 2000, we were speakers at a conference in Ottawa, Canada, where one of our elders resides. This man is now in his 80's and is blind. He came to the conference to support our generation in the native movement of cultural restoration. This man stood, 50 years ago, as a lone voice supporting the right for natives to worship Yahweh with their own languages, regalia and instruments. He had been severely abused by religious people in the church who thought everything the "Indians" did was demonic. At one point in the conference Grand-Chief Lynda Prince called him to the stage. A whole generation of First Nation's leaders, ages 30 to 55, knelt at his feet and repented for what the church had done to him. We also repented for what we, as young natives, had done to him by not showing him the honor that he was due as an elder and a spiritual leader. He had made many sacrifices so that we could follow in his footsteps, two generations later.

Although indigenous societies have undergone changes over the last decades one thing remains true to our people. The indigenous peoples of today still work hard developing programs that will further the well being of the elders. "The Choctaw Nation received funding in 1980 and started two nutrition sites to prevent isolation and loneliness among native elders. They know that it is important for the elders to gather together. In Fairbanks, the Native Associations Community Services Department Elder's Program provides multiple services to the elders including intergenerational activities and on-site health related services. The Pit River Native Association tries to help their elders live longer by providing anger and grief workshops and instruction on healthy preparation of meals. The Zuni natives opened an adult day care center for the elders so that the Zuni people do not have to put their family members in nursing homes."[5]

It is true that many have not been taught how to honor the elders in their families but it is never too late to begin. Here are some creative ways to begin the process. Ask yourself these questions.

1. "Who are the elders in my life? Begin with your family, then look to your friends, neighbors, church, and work place.

2. Who are the elders I might consult for wisdom?

3. What are my home, church, and workplace doing to honor the elders?

4. What am I doing to prepare the next generation to honor their elders?

5. How am I preparing myself to become an elder?"[6]

Here are some creative ideas that others are doing in order to honor their elders.

"Each fall the Picuris-Penasco community selects 13 elders for the Honoring Our Elders, A Celebration of Life Project.

Students from the Penasco High School and Middle School develop questions, train in oral interview techniques, and learn digital video and still camera skills. The interview crews travel to each elder's home and shoot about an hour of footage. The students participate in deciding which clips from each interview will go into the final hour-long documentary video featuring all of the elders. Students are given the opportunity to learn the video editing process. Each elder receives their own taped interview and a copy of the final project. The documentary is shown to the entire community, free of charge, at a local theatre. The project culminates in a festive, bridge-building community celebration honoring all the elders and the students that participated in the project. A dinner is served to the elders and their families, followed by an open community celebration, complete with an emcee, entertainment, gift baskets for the elders, and a dessert potluck table. Over 500 people attended the last celebration."[7]

"In Sarasota Florida, Pet Therapy, a local organization, honors the elders in a special way. Volunteers of all ages provide weekly visits to the local nursing homes with pets in tow. These volunteers are committed to being familiar with the residents of the nursing home by showing up at the same time every week. This gives the residents an opportunity to look forward to these visits and build a lasting relationship with these volunteers and their pets. The visits provide a positive effect on the resident's physical, emotional, and social interactions with others. The interaction with the animals has been shown to reduce blood pressure, increase sensory stimulation, inspire a sense of purpose, increase social interactions with the staff, and reduce loneliness by creating a sense of companionship. This program is a great way to teach younger volunteers the importance of honoring the elders."[8]

"Larry and Deborah Littlebird, founders and pastors of the White Dawn House, and the people of White Dawn House, honored the elders through their Listening Conferences recently held in New Mexico. The conferences brought together a diverse group of Pueblo, including spiritual elders from the 19 Pueblo tribes of New Mexico. These elders and native leaders share their voices, addressing the church about reconciliation topics. Pastors, ministry leaders and the Body of Christ (church people) were invited to participate as listeners. White Dawn House provides a platform in their conferences for the native peoples voices to be heard. The church of America, which is predominately Euro-American, honors the Native peoples by being willing to sit and listen to the voices of the native population that have been silenced for too long. The act of sitting quietly and humbly listening is a true act of restoration from the Christian church toward their native brothers and sisters. The Littlebirds believe that when people give of their time to sit down, be quiet, and fully listen to one another, the opportunity to start over is possible. This ministry is utilizing the wisdom of the elders to promote spiritual reconciliation and restoration between Pueblo Indian people and the church of America."[9]

In 2002, several leaders from around the United States joined together to honor John and Paula Sanford for their pioneering work in the area of healing and prophetic ministry. Some of us who could not attend sent letters of encouragement and thanks to the Sanfords, affirming them for the work that they have done in the Kingdom of Yahweh. "Some of the leaders washed the feet of the Sanfords, sang songs over them, and prayed prayers for them. Then some of the leaders presented themselves to the Sandfords and asked them to pray a prayer of impartation over them as they knelt at their feet. Previously, a sword had been placed in the hands of the Sanfords to honor them and they took that sword and placed it into the hands of the leaders from the younger generation. John and Paula, as well as many others, felt a "great shift in the heavenlies"—during that celebration of honor. Adonai had opened great doors of blessing.

Jim Goll, a speaker at the celebration, shared from Matthew 10. Matthew 10:40 states, "He who receives you receives Me, and He who receives Me receives Him who sent Me." Jim said the Body of Christ continually exclaims, "More Lord! More Lord!" and that one way that we can receive more of Yehshua is by receiving those He sends to us. This is also true of receiving the elders in our lives. We are missing out on so many blessings simply because we have not received the gifts the elders bring to us."[10]

Several years ago I (Qaumaniq) wanted to think of a way to honor the elder woman in my life, Dot Hathcock. She and her husband, Stanley, had recently celebrated their 50th wedding anniversary without much attention given to it. I decided to host a surprise 50th wedding celebration for them. I partnered with their children and grandchildren to have a renewal of their wedding vows. I wanted to do this as a gift, not just for Dot and Stanley, but for their whole family. I sent out invitations to all the family and friends and told them it was a surprise. We ordered a wedding cake, punch, and the whole works including a photographer. I raised money from our church congregation, who also attended, to purchase a plaque and buy them a nice gift. The children went through their photo albums and sneaked out significant pictures of them over their lifetime. I made a huge board with pictures of them that said "This Is Your Life- Stanley and Dot." We told them that they were coming to a church event and when they showed up at the door and walked into the church, everyone yelled "Surprise."

In a room, secluded from view were several secret guests that the Hathcocks had not seen for years, along with their brothers and sisters. We brought them out one at a time and they shared their memories of Stanley and Dot. There were many tears of joy. I then whisked Dot to a dressing room where we had a beautiful wedding dress and veil for her to put on. Her granddaughters and daughters were waiting for her as bridesmaids. Stanley, his son and grandsons, were standing up front as she came down the aisle, flowers in her hand, on the arm of a good friend that was like a second son to her. Her great-grandson was the ring bearer. I had picked out beautiful songs to be sung at their wedding renewal. The evening concluded with a reception and fun times for all.

Over the years I have continued to visit with Dot. Stanley passed away two years ago and she is now in an assisted living center. Every time I visit with her, she gets out the picture album, with the pictures of that day of celebration, and tells me how much that day meant to her. That memory of her coming down the aisle, looking up at the alter, and seeing her children and grandchildren before her with her handsome husband of 50 years waiting, will always be with her. Although that celebration came at a time in my own life when I was ill and it cost a lot in time and energy, I am so grateful that I sowed into Dot and her family. Like Dot, it has become one of my precious memories and it was the least I could do for the elder in my life.

We honor the elders because they are cherished by Yahweh. Because respect for elders is no longer regularly manifested in our society, we need to be more purposeful in expressing our honor. This can be accomplished by planning more special occasions and rituals to practice our honor. During the holidays, we can make a special effort to visit the elders of our church or to visit the local nursing homes in our area. In our family, we got the nursing home to give us the name of an elder that would not have family to visit. On Christmas day we took presents to this lady and spent time with her. She had problems with her memory and thought that we were her family. We played along, glad to give her some comfort on an otherwise lonely day for her.

> *"Because respect for elders is no longer regularly manifested in our society, we need to be more purposeful in expressing our honor."*

A wonderful token of honor that can be given to the elder in your life is to gather pictures of your elder from their birth until the present. Pick pictures of their life's adventures, values, and the people that were important to them and put them in an album for them to keep. When you visit them ask them to get out the album and share with you about the pictures. This can be a wonderful experience not only for your elder but for you as well. Your elder is full of wisdom, revelation, and entertaining stories. This can be a wonderful spiritually bonding experience.

Honoring the Elders

We often forget to sit with our elders and hear their stories that come through the guise of memories. My (Suuqiina's) auntie knew our ancestoral names back for 50 generations. Locked within her memory was the genealogy of our family. She would not allow herself to be recorded on tape because, according to the Inuit tradition, it should be passed down orally. She died last year and all that genealogy went with her. I wish I had had the foreknowledge to sit with her and memorize that wealth of information.

Author Alex Haley once commented, "The death of an old person is like the burning of a library." Now is the time to tap into the reservoir of stories because opportunities pass.

Here are some helpful hints to begin the process of showing your elders that you care.

1. "Ask your elder questions. Elders have a wealth of stories you have probably never heard. Sit and listen and let the elder do the talking. Ask questions such as, "What was the happiest day of your life?" "How did you meet your mate?" "What is the scariest thing that ever happened to you?"

2. Make yourself available through the phone. Purchase a phone for them that has large print buttons. Get yourself a toll-free number or purchase them a calling card so they can call you whenever they need to without the cost. Most elders are on a fixed income.

3. Call your elder regularly to let them know you care. Tell them you love them. Ask them for advice and help. This helps them to feel needed and valuable. Give them affirmation through compliments.

4. If your relationship with your elder is strained due to old hurts and misunderstandings, be willing to do the necessary work to clear up the past. Sort through what you are angry and hurt about and be willing to be honest. Share your memories and feelings with a counselor or a trusted friend. Be willing to forgive the past and move on but use appropriate boundaries for yourself, if the elder is difficult or unsafe.

5. Build new memories with walks in the park, sharing a craft or hobby, or by watching old movies.

6. Include your elder in family celebrations and holidays. Make their birthday a special and important day."[11]

7. "In many cultures and religious traditions, bowing is a way to show one's honor and reverence. Stand when your elder enters the room to show your respect and make a simple bow to your elder (an inner one will suffice if this would make your elder uncomfortable) when you greet or leave your elder."[12]

It is never too late to become a person of honor. If you have not been honoring your elders, now is the time to begin. We will all be elders someday and will experience the brevity of our time on earth, our personal frailty, and the winter season of our lives.

The Scriptures say that we are but a puff of smoke. We are here one day and then we are gone. Would that we would be known as a people who valued the elders and the contributions that they have made. Would that we would utilize the wealth of experience wrapped up in their precious souls. We can

Honoring the Elders

be people of honor and we can start by honoring the elders that the Creator has given to us as protocol gifts. Let us begin.

Warfare by Honor

Chapter Five

What's In A Name?

"A good name is preferable to great riches. Honor is better than silver and gold." Mishle (Proverbs) 22:1

"**P**resident Bill Clinton travels to South Korea to visit with President Kim Young Sam. While speaking publicly, the American President repeatedly refers to the Korean president's wife as Mrs. Kim. The South Korean officials are embarrassed."[1]

Why is the wife of Ghulam Hussein Sahib called Mr. Ghulam Hussein's Begum?

In a formal introduction, *Bapak Doctor Excellency Juanda Kusumaatmaja, Chief Accountant,* is presented to you. What does his name mean?

In the first instance, "President Clinton's advisers assumed that Koreans had the same naming tradition as the Japanese.

President Clinton had not been informed that, in Korea, wives retain their maiden names. President Kim Young Sam's wife was named Sohn Myong Suk. Therefore, her correct name was Mrs. Sohn. In Korea, the family name comes before the given name."[2]

Ghulam Hussein Sahib is a Pakistani. "The Pakistani equivalent of "Mr." Is *Sahib*. The female equivalent is (roughly) *Begum*. These titles follow the surname: Mr. Zia would be called Zia Sahib and Mrs. Hussein would be addressed as Hussein Begum. (However, she could more formally be referred to as Mr. Hussein's Begum.) These titles can also follow academic or job titles (Doctor Sahib or Director Sahib).

Another complexity is that some Pakistani names make sense only in context, relating a first name to a second name. If the name is broken down into each part, it conveys a different meaning. For example, the name Ghulam Hussein mean "slave of (the Islamic martyr) Hussein." To call him simply Ghulam is to address his as slave."[3]

What does *Juanda Kusumaatmaja* name mean? "The traditional Indonesian forms of Mr. And Madam, Mrs., or Miss are

Bapak = Mr. (this term precedes any other titles)

Ibu = Madam, Mrs., or Miss (any woman, married or unmarried)

These are used in front of an individual's name (e.g., Mr. Wowungan would be properly addressed as *Bapak* Wowungan.) Note that *Bapak* literally means "father," and *Ibu* is "mother."

In a formal introduction, the preferred sequence is

1. *Bapak* or *Ibu*

2. Academic title, if any

3. Honorific, if any (a title of nobility)

4. The individual's given and family name

5. Business or political title.

Thus, a formal introduction for a male executive named Juanda (given name) Kusumaatmaja (family name) could be as long as *Bapak Doctor His Excellency* Juanda Kusumaatmaja, *Chief Accountant.*"[4]

> "*Everyone takes pride in their name and will usually defend it's honor whenever necessary.* "
>
> ౫ఎ

Everyone takes pride in their name and will usually defend it's honor whenever necessary. Many, if not most, of the First Nation's people were dishonored by the replacement of their honorable names with dishonorable ones (e.g. The Lakota were called *Souix* by the immigrants. *Souix* means "snake," an obvious slander upon an entire people group. The name *Apache* means "my enemy." This is one of the worst kinds of dishonor that can happen to anyone. Yaweh Himself gave a commandment not "to take His name in vain" nor to "replace it with another (see Rev.3:8)."

Sometimes a name will mean something in one culture and something completely different in another. Sometimes the difference will be honorable in one culture and dishonorable in another.

"The Thom McAn Company traditionally sells shoes with a nearly-illegible "Thom McAn" signature printed inside and near the bottom of the shoe. But when it tried to sell footwear in Bangladesh, a riot ensued in which more than fifty people were injured. It seems that the "Thom McAn" signature looked like Arabic script for "Allah." Outraged Muslims decided that Thom McAn was trying to get Bangladeshis to desecrate the name of God by walking on it—an insult in any culture, but especially in Bangladesh, where the foot is considered unclean."[5]

A name, its order, etc. may seem unimportant to many Americans because Americans generally pride themselves on their informality. This is not, however, seen as a virtue in most other places of the world. Such informality has contributed to the reputation of the "ugly American." This lack of honoring the protocol of naming can be both costly to the business community, and most negative to believers attempting to share their faith.

"Mexican naming customs differ as well. When a woman marries, she keeps her maiden name and adds her husband's name after the word *de* (of): After marrying Tino Martinez, Maria Gonzales becomes Maria Gonzales Martinez. When children are born, the name order is as follows: given name, father's family name, mother's family names. Tino and Maria's child Anita is named Anita Martinez Gonzales."[6]

Most cultures have rituals for the naming of a child. These rituals can be elaborate or simple depending upon the culture.

Yeshua was named by Elohim through the angel Gabriel and revealed to Mariam.

An angel also revealed John (Yohanan) the Baptist's name to his father.

Many children are given names related to their immediate family or to continue a family name. Some names were given as names of honor or for positions within a tribe. Names can have, and ought to have, a powerful effect upon a person and be something of pride and honor. It becomes one of the most important elements of a person's identity.

In the Hebrew culture the naming of a child often accompanied the act of circumcision. "This happened in Yeshua's case (see Luke 2:21) So important was the birth and the naming ceremony that sometimes parents' names were changed. Father became "father of x," and mother became "mother of y."[7] It may be important to some to restore the name *Yeshua,* which was replaced by *Jesus* after the letter 'j' was added to the English alphabet in 1576.

It would be honoring to the Hebrew culture to retain the original name of the One who will give us all new names in a great heavenly reunion of believers. In any case, the name *Jesus* was never heard in Israel until after the late 1500's.

It might be helpful to note that when one visits a foreign country, that person's name is retained. We are still Qaumaniq and Suuqiina even when we visit another country where another language is spoken. The biblical names did not have to be changed and, in fact, we may have lost significant understanding by not retaining the original names as they contained within their meanings revelation about that person, culture, or passage of scripture. It is possible to purchase scriptures with the original names restored.

The words God and Lord are not proper names as such but rather descriptions. Yaweh has revealed Himself by many names such as, El Elyon, El Shaddai, Adonai, El Olam, Elohim, etc.

The Hebrew root of the name Elohim means "justice." This is the name of the Creator. In Bereshith (1 Moshe or Genesis) it reveals that Elohim created the heavens and the earth. They were created by 'Justice.' Later it says that Elohim commented upon His creation and said, "It is good." The Hebrew says He said "It is right." When 'Justice' creates something it is right. Trees are right for bird's nests, oceans are right for fish, ground is right for ground hogs, etc.

You might find it interesting that in Bereshith chapter two, when Elohim created male and female, the name *Adonai* is added and precedes the name Elohim. The Hebrew root of Adonai is mercy, therefore, when man and woman were created 'Justice,' preceded by 'Mercy,' created them. This would be consistent with the scripture that states "mercy triumphs over judgment."

In Galatians 6:7 it says, "Do not be led astray: Elohim (Justice) is not mocked, for whatever a man sows, that he shall also reap." Knowing that Elohim means justice causes this verse to make sense and brings another level of understanding and gravity to the context of the verse. The truth remains that Elohim, Justice, will never be mocked. Justice prevails, always!

In Revelation 3:8 the Messenger says, "….(you) have guarded My Word (Torah), and have not denied My Name." One of the Greek renditions of "have not denied My Name" reads "have not substituted My Name for (or with) another." It can be clearly understood that the Anti-Christ (where anti does not mean "against" but "another" or "different" one) will not likely use the name Yeshua since the He is not known by that name but by the "substituted" one. Anti-Christ will use the name that is familiar to most people. Knowing and using the original name can be a protection against deception and an ally for discernment.

"It is time that Christians reclaime the many beautiful names of the One Creator God in native languages instead of falling into Satan's trap and destroying them. We should reclaim those names and wash the dung of corruption off of them instead of giving them up to Satan. We must cast off the corruption that Satan has thrown on the many beautiful names of God in native languages.

Instead of destroying and ridiculing the native names of the Creator God, we should help preserve them as a legacy for these peoples. It is their legacy of God's enduring interest, involvement and care for their culture and people! Christians should cease representing Jesus as the Son of a foreign God of a foreign people, especially if these foreigners had never shown concern for nor had any involvement in the lives or culture of the natives. We should instead introduce Jesus as the Son of **their creator God**.[8]

In many cultures, the names given new borns is so important that elaborate ceremonies were conducted as naming ceremonies.

The Navajo First Nations chant a song over a newborn to ensure health, harmony, and prosperity. This chant is called the Blessing Way and tells a story from the Navajo people's past. Every time a child is born the Blessing Way song is sung reinforcing the blessing and importance of every child and adult in the Navajo Nation.

"The Hopi Indians live in the American Southwest. Today, as in former times, a Hopi grandmother on its father's side leads the preparations for the newborn child's "naming ceremony." This is a very important event, held twenty days after birth. Until then, a Hopi baby has no name.

Before dawn on the naming day, the baby receives its name in a ceremony at which the father sees his new child for the first time. Then, as the sun rises, the mother and the father's mother present the baby to the sunrise and repeat the name."[9]

"Among the Tsalagi (Cherokee), the number seven is sacred. Therefore, on a Tsalagi baby's seventh day of life, traditionalists in the tribe still take him/her to the Long Man (river). There the medicine person prays for the baby while holding the newborn over the water. The baby is offered to the water seven times but does not touch it until the mother wets her finger and gently places them on the baby."[10] This naming protocol is quite similar to the christening ceremony amongst many religions.

In the Hebrew culture, the mother stayed at home for thirty-three days (sixty-six in the case of a girl baby) to make ready the customary offerings. Usually a lamb, along with a pigeon or dove, was offered as a sin offering to restore a woman's fellowship with Yahweh (see Lev.12). This sin offering shows the woman had become ritually unclean through childbirth but not an actual defilement. In the case of a firstborn child, redemption money of five shekels had to be paid because, since the preservation of the Jewish firstborn at the original Passover, all first-born children belong to Yahweh (see Num.18:15-16).

If your heritage has lost it's naming ceremony or your family has not developed a naming protocol, it is not too late to begin. The naming ceremony is a traditional bonding time amongst the families of a newborn. It is important.

Maybe it has become easier to dishonor someone's name because we don't honor the naming ceremonies of others. Even the act of giving a "nickname" to someone maybe a subtle act of dishonoring their given name. Protocol requires everyone to understand what a person's relationship might be to his/her own name. For many cultures a person's name is one of the most important and serious things about them.

For many First Nation's People, who were taken from their homes and placed in residential schools, one of the greatest indignities was the removal of their native names for Euro-American ones. The new names had no meaning for them other than a daily reminder that their culture and their native names were somehow less than what was expected or validated by their Euro-American oppressors.

"People walk in shame whose names have been dishonored."

Many First Nation People have had to use two names to participate in modern society, a Euro-American and a native one. Most often native names couldn't be used for business, governmental, or social purposes. People walk in shame whose names have been dishonored. Some indigenous tribes will not reveal their native names accept amongst their own people (i.e.Blackfoot). It is their way of preserving the honor and power of their native name and status.

The scriptures record many instances where people's names were changed, some in a good way, others not. Abram was changed, by Yahweh, to Abraham; Sarai to Sarah, Jacob to Israel, and Saul to Paul, amongst others. Some names were changed in order to effect a change in the identity or perception of others about those who were renamed.

In Daniel 1:1,2 we read of some Hebrew captives and their captors, the Babylonians, determination to corrupt them. The Prince of the Babylonian eunuchs determined to impose the character and spirit of Babylon on Daniel, Hananiah, Mishael, and Azariah. He gave them Babylonian names, all of which were related to the occult practices common to those captors.

To Daniel, whose name meant "Yahweh is My Judge," the eunuch gave the name Belteshazzar which meant " Baal, Protect His Life."

To Hananiah, "Yahweh is Gracious," was given the name Shadrach meaning "Under the Command of Aku," the Babylonian moon god.

To Mishael, "Who is like Yahweh?" he gave the name Meshach, "Who is Like Aku?"

To Azariah, "Helped by Yahweh," he gave the name Abednego, "Servant of Nego," a Babylonian sun god.

In spite of these dishonoring name changes, these Hebrew captives determined a different course of thinking and behavior for themselves. Daniel "purposed in his heart that he would not defile himself (Dan.1:8)." While being called by dishonorable names that were intended to change their self-image, these men remained faithful to the honorable names of their origin. Yahweh honored them by prospering them physically, mentally, and emotionally. It is a biblical account with a great and miraculous end.

The protocol of the naming ceremony is beautiful in every culture. It is one of the most important events in a child's life. The names given have great meaning and have a profound effect upon the direction of a person's life.

Our Creator can help us live above and beyond the borders of prejudice, stereotypes, and negative cliches. We can honor other cultures by understanding their ways, their preferences, and actively seeking to avoid any dishonor to them. Dishonor can injure and hurt, sometimes beyond repair.

A story is told about Alexander the Great. He had conquered the known world and was reviewing his troops while in Egypt. A nineteen-year-old deserter was brought before him and everyone expected the lad to be killed on the spot. Alexander asked the boy his name and he answered, "Alexander." It is said that Alexander the Great became furious and shouted to the boy, "Change your character or change your name!"

Our character is bound up with the meaning and purpose of our name.

"Healing is about learning to act in a good way. Healing is also about taking responsibility."[11] (Patricia Monture-Angus, Law Professor, Mohawk Nation)

What is your name? What does it mean? What meaning does it have to you and how has it affected your life? If you could choose another name, what would it be and why? What are your family's names and what do they mean? If you were named "after" someone, what kind of person was she/he?

> *And Jacob asked Him, saying, "Please let me know your Name." And He said, "Why do you ask about My Name?" and He blessed him there.* Genesis 32:29

> *Then shall those who fear Yahweh speak to one another, and Yahweh listen and hear, and a book of remembrance be writ - ten before Him, of those who fear Yahweh, and those who think upon **His Name**.* Malachi 3:16

Warfare by Honor

Chapter Six

Rights of Passage

In the native cultures of the world, when young men and women are ready to take their part as adults in their tribes, they are given a special ceremony. In order to become an adult in these cultures, one is expected to know the wisdom and the ways of their people. Many times this is taught through the oral tradition, sharing of songs, dances, and stories of the elders.

Young men and women are expected to learn the sacred times, places, and things that are holy to their people. In the native cultures, children do not enter into adult life in a haphazard way. Moving from childhood to adulthood is purposeful and full of meaning.

The Dene

"When a Dene (Navajo) girl reaches puberty, the whole family gathers to prepare for the ceremony that will mark this transition from one part of her life to another. The affirmation and initiation into adult Dene society is called "Kin nal dah" which means "she becomes a woman."

The girl is prepared for the ceremony by her aunt and grandmother who tie her hair into a certain style of bun. The medicine man then performs the 'Blessing Way' ceremony that lasts for four days.

At noon, on the first day, the girl runs to the east about one or two miles with other runners following behind her. No one is allowed to outrun the girl. A Dene belief is that anyone who outruns her will grow old, faster than the girl. This act is repeated up to the third day.

On the third day, the medicine man continues the ceremony. The people gather all day, eat and wait for the all-night ceremony to begin. At sundown, a special cake is prepared in a pit that has been dug in the ground. The medicine man blesses the cake with songs and sprinkles corn pollen on the cake in the four directions. It is then covered and a fire is built on top of it and it is left to cook all night long.

On the last morning, the girl runs to the east one final time. When she comes back from her run she is laid on the ground, on a blanket. The women elders stretch her out and she is massaged from head to toe. It is a Dene belief that they are shaping her into a beautiful woman. After this she stands up and they stretch her hair so that she will have long hair. This trait is important to the Dene.

The elders then counsel her about becoming a woman and tell her the duties of a wife and mother. The cake is then taken out of the ground and given to everyone. It is believed that everyone who eats this cake will be strengthened in mind, body, and spirit."[1]

The Apache

"The Apache puberty rite is called the "Sunrise Ceremony." The ceremony dramatizes the creation story. The medicine man chooses the time and place to hold the ceremony. If it happens to rain, the Apache do not call off the ceremony instead it becomes a sacred test to the belief of the girl. It also proves her ability to withstand hardship and to maintain control of her destiny.

There are four poles lashed together in the four scared directions that are decorated with artifacts and symbols. The entrance is to the East. A tarp is spread out on the earth with soft blankets for the girl. In front of the blankets there will be a basket filled with goodies. There will also be a basket with a pollen mixture in it that is used to bless the girl later in the ceremony.

The girl always faces east, so her family will always be on her right (south) and her sponsors will be on her left (north). The medicine man and singers will stand directly behind her. It is improper for anyone to get between the girl and the sun or to prevent the sunbeams from shining on her.

In the Apache way, having a period does not make a girl a woman. She must earn the right to be recognized as a woman before the elders, the community and the spiritual world.

For four holy days and nights she is unable to wash, scratch, or drink, except through an anointed tube. She must hold her hands exactly right, she must not slump in posture, her head must be straight, and her cane must strike the ground exactly right. This will test her physical stamina, discipline, and social skills.

The four-day ceremony begins with a purifying sweat bath. The sponsor then sends a gift of prepared food to the girl's camp. As the sun sets, the medicine man sets out the girls feathers, shell, pick stick, drinking tube, scarf, buckskin and cane. He gives her instructions while her sponsor affixes these items. As the sun sets the girl begins to prepare for her dance.

Before sunrise, on the second day, the tribe is busy preparing for the long day and night. All must be prepared before the girl begins her dance at sunrise. She begins her dance with an experienced friend who has already gone through her own ceremony. The medicine man stands behind the girls and leads the singers in songs of beauty and goodness. The girl must dance to each of the songs and to the complete satisfaction of the people that attend the ceremony. She dances hour after hour staring into the sun.

She cannot run to the toilet when she needs to go, she can not sit down when she is tired, or move to the shade when she is hot. She must continue to dance. The longer she dances, the higher the sun rises, and the hotter she gets in her buckskin.

After the songs are sung, she will kneel and sway while four more songs are sung. She must hold her hands in an acceptable way, at an acceptable height, and sway from north to south. In this stage of the ceremony, the elder women or her sponsor will correct her to assure that she is doing the ceremony in the right way and with honor. This exercise is physically challenging. After hours of strenuous movement it ends, and the girl then get a massage. The massage is done by the placing of a foot on the girl's sore muscles. While lying down, the girl has to strain to keep her head high in the required position. This is also physically challenging. This is done while four songs are sung.

Once completed, her cane is set out and she is required to dance and run around her cane so fast that no one can catch her. Each time she succeeds, the medicine man moves the cane further east so she has to run further and faster.

The basket of blessings is then dumped on the girl's head. This basket is called the burden basket. As soon as the medicine man dumps it on her, the people from every direction begin to snatch the gifts. The Apache are not accustomed to this feeling of being surrounded and grabbed at by so may people, so it is very uncomfortable for them. She then is required to resume her dancing.

She must continue to dance while everyone blesses her, then the medicine man blesses her. This can seem to take forever, especially if many people attend her ceremony. The medicine man sprinkles a handful of pollen over her head and then prayers are offered. The girl must continue dancing through all the prayers. The girl then offers healing prayers for those who are sick and need a touch of healing.

After the blessings are finished, they return to their camps for more singing and dancing and to prepare for the night ceremony. The night time ceremony begins at dusk. No artificial lights are allowed. A fire is prepared and the Apache stand, with their backs to the fire, looking out at the darkness. The ceremony begins with singing and the girl will appear with her friends and dance at the edge of the firelight. The dancing will continue until dawn.

The medicine man will be up before dawn mixing a paint mixture. Various dignitaries will go to the mixture, add a drop of water and stir in a few more prayers. The girl's friend will arrive and accompany her in dancing for a good part of the morning. The medicine man then instructs the girl's friend to leave and the girl dances over to her male sponsor and extends the bottom of her cane. The male sponsor grabs the end of the cane and holds it. He follows the girl around the dance ground to enter through the south side. The sponsor then dances on the north side of the girl.

Once this has been done, the painting of the girl begins. The paint is brushed and patted around the girl's head. Some are painted by the medicine man, some by the sponsors, and some by the people attending. After she is painted, the girl is given the basket of paint and she carries it with her sponsor, who dips the brush into the paint and showers the crowd with the paint as a symbol of blessings. When the basket of paint is empty, the crowd dances through the portal in each of the four, sacred directions.

The people then return to the camp where the girl will remain for another day where she will do good deeds. She is expected to prosper and in two years her ceremony will come to a close with a give away ceremony. She acknowledges the generosity of her sponsors by presenting them with many gifts.

This ceremony teaches the girl that hardships in life will come but that she can do more and endure more than she perceives her ability and endurance to be. It also teaches her about her interdependence on the community in which she lives."[2]

The Yup'ik

"In the Yup'ik tradition, young teenage girls were given their own house or room within the home. They were waited on, hand and foot, and forbidden to work. They had to sit quietly, in seclusion, and wait for the process that would transform them from a girl to a woman."[3]

The Lakota

"Among the Lakota, the puberty rites for girls is considered to be one of seven sacred rites from the Great Spirit. A huge feast is held for the girl. The medicine person sings a song for the girl and instructs her in her adult duties. A sacred eagle feather is then placed into her hair to symbolize her new role in the tribe."[4]

The Choctaw

"In the Choctaw culture, when a girl comes of age, her family sponsors a coming of age ceremony. The girls are given three days of private instruction. On the first day, the male tribal elders meet with her and tell her how important she is as a young woman to her tribe and the importance of the role of women in the government of the people.

Next, the women of the tribe take her out into the swamps to teach her about herbs, medicine, and craft making. They teach her about foods and cooking.

On the fourth day, her father takes her to the grocery store to shop for the poor people in the tribe. She will buy food and take it to them to honor them. The poor are invited to the ceremony and asked to pray for the girl. This teaches the girl to take care of the poor and to remember them.

When time for the ceremony comes, the girl has to wait on the elders to remind her to respect her elders. She is in her regalia (native outfit) that she has made herself and worked on for many years. This is comprised of jewelry, dress, and moccasins. She has been fasting and praying. She will then do an honor dance to the songs of her people. When the dancing ends, she will pray for the people that have lined up in front of her.

After this she will go and change her clothes. She takes the regalia, she has worked on for so many years, and gives it to different women in the tribe who have been role models to her. In so doing, she learns to hold lightly to things and to always give to others your very best. This is the native way."[5]

The Vision Quest

"Many tribes mark a boy's puberty with a ritual known as a vision quest. In this process, the boy goes off alone to seek a Guardian Spirit to protect and guide him throughout his life. This spirit gives the boy skills and special gifts such as the power to heal. Unlike the girl's onetime puberty ceremony, vision quests can be repeated during the life of the boy become man. Each tribe has a different type of ceremony called the vision quest, but most of the tribes begin with a purifying bath in a sweat lodge.

If the boy does not receive his vision, he has to return home and will have to wait until the next year and try again. Once the vision is received, the medicine man will interpret the vision. In some tribes, when a boy reaches puberty and receives his vision, he will receive a new name.

In some tribes, the men take the boy out into the wilderness. He will do a sweat with the elders and then fast for three days alone. After the three days, he will seek counsel from the elders to interpret the spiritual experience that he has gone through during the three days alone. Many times this ceremony will enlighten the boy on his purpose in life, and powers will be given to him that will help him to be a blessing to his tribe."[6]

The Bar Mitzvah

"In the Jewish culture a boy is recognized as a man at thirteen years of age. He is then considered a "son of the law." In the Scriptures (Luke 2:41-49) where Yeshua was left behind at the Temple, it shows that He was leaving His childhood. It was the last time that He would attend Passover as a child. In the Jewish culture, the quality of a person's questions is seen as the measure of understanding. This value is reflected, when we read in the scriptures, at how the scribes marveled at the questions of Yeshua during this meeting in the temple.

Only after age thirteen does a boy qualify to become one of ten men that is required to constitute a synagogue. Until a son is the age of thirteen, a father is responsible for his son's actions and children are not required to observe the commandments. This explains the famous Jewish quote, "Until the thirteenth year I talk to my son about God; after his Bar mitzvah I talk to God about my son."

A Jewish girl becomes a woman at age twelve. This day holds as great a joy as the day of one's wedding. For girls this is called the Bat Mitzvah.

The coming of age in Jewish society does not mean that one is an adult in every sense of the word. It is, however, the proper age for the fulfillment of the commandments. It is the age at which a person becomes responsible for his/her own actions. It is the time of crossing out of the fantasy world of childhood into a realistic view of the adult world. It is a time to decide what kind of person one wants to be and what path in life one wants to take."[7]

"In the present life of the Jewish people, the Bar Mitzvah and Bat Mitzvah are typically celebrated with a meal attended by family and friends. During the meal, speeches are given, by those in attendance, to encourage the young person to pursue good values and spirituality. On the Shabbat (Sabboth service) following the birthday, the young person is called to the Torah (Scriptures) during the services at the synagogue to recite the Torah portion and the blessing on the Haftorah."[8]

As you read through these stories of rites of passage for different people groups, you can probably see how these symbolic rituals can be redemptive stories that point the way to Yeshua. Though as believers, we might not be able to embrace all these ceremonies offer, we do not have to throw away these ceremonies entirely in order to pursue Christian faith. These ceremonies can be adapted to not only fit our faith, but to also enrich our faith.

It saddens us that many in the American culture have lost this wonderful way to bless our children. How different our lives might have been had we received this blessing. We now live in a society that has lost this ceremonial marker of time. We believe that this has contributed to the development of gangs and the gang mentality. The generation of young people, commonly known as Generation X, is looking for identity and ceremonies that give foundation to their lives. We are not saying that all the behaviors of the gangs are good but we are saying that the intent to develop a way of belonging, to something and someone out side of ones self, is normal and admirable. Perhaps if we restore some of the ceremonial markers for this generation, it would be helpful and edifying to them.

Several years ago as I (Qaumaniq) began to study the Hebraic roots of my Christian faith, I learned about the Bar Mitzvah. I longed to give that blessing to my sons.

One of our sons was sixteen and one was already twenty. I decided to put together blessing parties for them, to release them into manhood. I held the parties for them on their birthdays in the same year. I sent out invitations to people that were special to each of them and our family. I asked each person to bring a written blessing letter that would include, good memories with my son, what they saw in their lives that was a gift to them, and what they would like to see for my son. I asked them to write a special scripture for my son.

At the celebration, we were seated in a circle, so that we could look at one another. Each person looked at our son and read the blessing out loud to them. It was a time of laughter and tears. At the end of the letters, our son stood in the middle of the circle and the men came and laid their hands on him. They called him into his manhood and prayed prayers of blessing over him.

Later that week, I took all of the blessing letters and put them in a book for him so that he could pull it out and read these blessings whenever he needed encouragement and direction. I also filmed the whole blessing party so that we would have a record of this important day. It was an incredible time that they will never forget. It was a day to celebrate their lives and the gift that they bring to life simply by being who Yahweh made them to be.

I am so glad that I took the time to do this. I wish every child had this gift and could celebrate their rites of passage from childhood to adulthood.

It is never too late to give this blessing to a friend or family member. I had my rites of passage party in my forties, after my sons had celebrated their coming of age. Several of my friends gathered to celebrate my Bat Mitzvah. It was held during a dark night of my soul, when I was struggling with a life threatening chronic illness. I believe that the blessings that were spoken over me that day allowed me to persevere and enabled me to choose life. Blessings break curses, even generational curses, and the blessings from my family and friends broke the power of the enemy over my life.

If you have children, please consider re-establishing this honorable practice in your family. We can restore the ancient ruins and rebuild the walls of blessing if each of us will do our part. It is never to late to begin and we can change the destinies of our family and friends through these important practices.

Chapter Seven

The Protocol of Weddings

Most cultures of the world have traditions concerning courtship and marriage.

In biblical times, in the Jewish culture, young couples did not decide whom they would marry. However, this did not mean that parents did not consider their children's choices (see Genesis 24: 58).

"A friend who attends the bridegroom (see John 3:29) would negotiate on behalf of the intended bridegroom and his father to a representative of the bride's father. Arrangements would then be made for the 'mohar,' which is work compensation to be paid to the woman's family. Also, a dowry had to be paid to the bride's father. When it was not possible for the groom to pay a dowry, due to lack of funds, the groom could work for hire for the bride's father (see Genesis 29:18).

The bride would wear part of the coins from the dowry in a headdress. This became a symbol, like a wedding ring, and the loss of a coin like this (see Luke 15:8-10) could be the cause of great concern.

It was common to marry within one's own kin (see Genesis 24:3-4), to prevent marriage with people that worshipped idols. Marriage with close relatives such as sisters or brothers was forbidden.

Once these arrangements were made final, there was a betrothal that was much more serious and binding than engagement in our contemporary society. Betrothals could only be broken by a legal document, like a divorce. The betrothal period lasted about a year and during this time the groom prepared a home for the bride while the bride prepared her wedding garments. The family members would also prepare for the wedding. The formal betrothal would commence when the groom gave a present to the bride and said to her, "By this, thou art set apart for me according to the laws of Moses and of Israel."

The wedding involved a legal document and was not necessarily a religious ceremony. The participants would dress up, the bride being attired in the fashion of a queen (see Rev. 21:2). She was bathed and would have her hair braided with precious stones. Sometimes the family would borrow the stones if they could not afford their own (see Psalm 45:14-15; Isaiah 61:10; Ezekiel 16:11-12).

The girls' who had dressed her, accompanied her as companions or bridesmaids. The dressing up for the wedding was so important that it was the most memorable part to the ceremony see (Isaiah 61:10).

The bridegroom was also dressed in his best and was accompanied by the friend of the bridegroom (see John 3:29). At the end of the day, there was a procession in which the bridegroom set out from his home to fetch his bride from her parents home. During this time, the bride would be wearing a veil and at some point the veil would be taken off and laid on the shoulder of the bridegroom. The declaration would then be made, "The government shall be upon his shoulder." Then the procession would leave the bride's home to the couple's new home and the dark roadway would be lit up with oil lamps held by the wedding guests (see Matthew 25:1-13).

During the processional, there was singing along the way and the bride would often dance (see Jeremiah 16:9; Song of Songs 6:13). It was traditional for the bride and groom to enter under a canopy as they arrived at the house. Once they entered the house, they presided over a wedding feast at which they spent a lot of time eating and drinking (see Song of Solomon 2:4).

It was at one such traditional wedding feast where Yeshua preformed his first miracle by turning the water into wine. The feast often lasted for seven days (see Judges 14:12) and sometimes even longer. The guests were also at the wedding to witness that the marriage had been consummated (see Genesis 29:22-23); the bloodstained bed coverings were displayed to prove that the bride had been a virgin (see Deut. 22: 13-21). It seems, by reading the scriptures, that the veil must not have been removed until the wedding was consummated since Jacob did not know that he had married Leah, instead of Rachel, until daylight (see Genesis 29:23). During the celebrations, Yahweh's blessings were requested for the couple. In wealthy or royal families, guests were provided with wedding clothes (see Matt. 22:12)."[1]

In many First Nations cultures, the parents arranged marriages. Girls married young and they made their own regalia for weddings.

"In the southwestern tribes, older male relatives wove wedding dresses for the brides. In the Hopi, the brides had two dresses that were prepared for their weddings. One dress is for the wedding and one is for her burial. During the courting stage, if a Hopi boy wanted a girl to become his bride, he would make a bundle for her and leave it on the doorstep. If she accepted the clothes it meant that she accepted him. A Hopi wedding takes a very long time to prepare. Before the wedding, the bride spends four days grinding corn. She does it with other female relatives who grind the corn with her."[2]

"In the culture of the Dene, the groom must pay a price for the bride. It is shameful to marry without receiving a bride price. To be paid for was an honorable tradition. It meant the marriage would get off to a good start.

In Dene weddings, the marriage takes place late in the day because their tradition dictates that the sun must reach a particular position in the western sky, at sundown, before they can start the ceremony. Inside a Hogan, the groom faces south and follows the path of the sun. He sits on the floor and his family sits by him to the north.

The Dene bride carries a shallow basket that has been woven out of yucca with a layer of cornmeal mush inside. The bride sits on the right side of the groom and her family sits on her right side. Her basket of cornmeal and the wedding gifts are placed on the floor as well.

At some point in the ceremony, the bride and groom wash their hands in a cup of water that has been brought for them. Then the relative in charge of the basket turns it so the east end of the line faces the couple. The bridegroom takes a pinch of the cornmeal mush with his fingers, eats it, and then the bride does the same, making sure that she dips her fingers into the same place that he dipped his fingers. Sometimes the basket is passed around to all the guests. Whoever eats the last bit of cornmeal mush gets to keep the basket."[3]

"The Iroquois women are the ones that make the arrangements for their children's marriages. When a mother feels that her son is ready to be married, she will find a suitable girl and negotiate a bride price with the girl's mother. The ultimate decision belongs to the mothers and not to the children.

The wedding ceremony of the Iroquois is very simple. The marriage is announced and the following day the bride's mother or maternal grandmother goes to the house of the groom's maternal grandmother and takes her some wedding cakes, carried in a basket. The offering of the cakes shows that the bride's family approves of the marriage. If the groom's family approves of the marriage, they eat the cakes and put meat into the empty basket.

Sometimes the groom will move into his wife's family house for awhile, sometimes for two years, and he will hunt and fish under the authority of his mother-in-law. She will always be offered a portion of what he has caught. Sometimes he may give her all of it."[4]

Warfare by Honor

"The Oglala (Sioux) sometimes dress in their best regalia and paint their face in bright colors when they are wooing their bride to be. The will put on a courting robe and walk in front of the tipi where the woman he wants to marry lives. She will then come out of her tipi and he will wrap the courting robe around the two of them.

The woman's family will then ask him to sit with them. If the woman smiles at the man it means that she is willing to accept him. If she turns her back on him it means that she rejects him. If she accepts him, she will offer him first water and then food. She will also make a pair of moccasins for him that she decorates herself. When he puts the moccasins on they are formally engaged.

The groom's oldest and closet relative will then visit the bride's family and negotiate the bride price. Sometimes the negotiations will take place over several meetings and it is common to have feasts that include family and friends.

Sometimes the groom plays the native courting flute to his bride in order to woo her to himself.

The day of the ceremony the bride will put on her bridal regalia and paint her hair, face, or hands. The groom will bring the bride price to her tipi. As soon as the bride price is delivered, she will take him by the right hand and lead him into her tipi. She will seat him in a place of honor and place moccasins on his feet. This concludes the marriage ceremony.

Some First Nations groups observe so few customs that two people are married simply by deciding to live together. Other groups have awesome marriage ceremonies that will last for days."[5]

The Protocol of Weddings

"The Tlingit, a Pacific Northwest tribe, have their spouses chosen for them by their parents. The courtship begins with the boy's family offering many valuable gifts that represent how much the family thinks the bride is worth. When the gifts are accepted then the marriage preparations begin. The groom and bride's families also exchange gifts.

Marriage among the Pacific Northwest Natives is celebrated with a potlatch. This is a celebration that includes gift giving and a big feast of tribal foods. At the potlatch there is also music and dancing and they can last for several days. At the potlatch, gifts are given to the guests."[6]

"Amongst the Ojibway, a relationship between a man and a woman is described by the word 'weedjeewaugun.' The word means companion and 'he or she who walks with.'"[7]

"A native woman in Guatemala has four marriage customs to respect. The first one is the open door. The second one is a commitment to the parents, when the girl has accepted her groom. This custom is very important. The third is the ceremony in which the bride and groom exchange their vows. The forth is the wedding called the despedida.

In order to marry in Guatemala, the boy will tell his parents that he likes a certain girl. The boy and his parents then speak to the village representative and tell him that he wants to ask this certain girl to marry him. A door is opened, by the village representative, for the young man's parents and the young man. This usually takes place at about four in the morning.

Girls get married at about fourteen years of age and have babies by age fifteen. When the request is made to the father of the girl, it is the custom that the father not agree to the marriage at first. It is customary for the village representative to go back many times to plead with the girl's parents. After the door is opened, meaning that the groom's proposal has been accepted, the parents sit together and the bride's parents tell the groom's parents their daughter's good points. Then the groom's parents tell the bride's parents their son's good and bad traits. If the door is still opened and the groom is accepted, then he may call upon the bride on Sundays. When he comes by, he must bring a present for her parents.

If the girl does not like the boy, she will not talk to him. When he comes, she will just keep doing her work around the house. The family will wait fifteen days to see if she will talk to him. If she talks to him, he is accepted into the family as her groom. If she does not talk to him, they let him know that the marriage is not going to take place."[8]

"In the Indonesian culture, wedding attendance is very important. Attendance shows that people care and that the person attending has respect for the bride, groom, and their families. Wedding invitations can be very extravagant. Instead of gifts, the guests give money. The guests are then given a gift at the wedding so that it is not necessary for the bride and groom to send "thank you" notes .

The path to the reception hall will be lined with members of the extended families and most often they will be wearing traditional dress. Young men and women, holding a chain of flowers, will follow the family members. This is called the pagar ayu or the fence of beauty.

Dancers, in traditional dress, will proceed the bride and groom in the wedding processional and will give a traditional dance performance. Once the wedding party is seated, a representative of each family will address the guests to thank them for coming to the wedding."[9]

The Protocol of Weddings

"In the Chinese wedding, to prepare for her launching from her family at the event of her marriage, the Chinese bride-to-be will cease from her ordinary routine and live in seclusion in a separate part of the house from her family. Her closest friends will join her during this time. The young women will sing laments to mourn the separation of her from her family.

A week before the wedding, the family of the groom will go, without the groom, to the house of the bride and bring gifts in red containers. Red symbolizes happiness and prosperity for the Chinese.

The baskets of gifts from the groom, will all be carried by males. The bride accepts the gifts and takes them off to another room, where she will sort through the gifts. About half of the gifts are placed back in the containers and given back to the groom's family.

Three days before the wedding, the bride's family returns the favor by taking gifts to the family of the groom. Females of the bride's immediate family carry these baskets. Some of the baskets contain personal clothes and grooming supplies of the bride. By accepting these items, the groom's family is accepting her into their house. On her wedding day, when she moves in, all of her personal items and possessions will already be at the groom's home. Again the gifts are sorted through and half of the items are returned.

The day before the wedding, the groom will be responsible for the installation of the bridal bed. After the bed is installed, children are invited onto the bed as a sign of fertility. For this same reason the bed is covered with red dates, oranges, lotus seeds, peanuts, pomegranates and other fruit.

The children get to gather the fruit. On the morning of the wedding, the groom and his parents go to the house of the bride. At this time the groom and bride will serve tea to both sets of parents, while kneeling down in front of them to show their respect.

On the day of the wedding, great care is given in preparing the bride for the wedding processional. One tradition is a hair dressing ritual. Then the bride waits for the wedding processional from the bride's house. She is carried on a sedan chair to the home of the groom. Firecrackers are set off just before the bride arrives. A red mat is placed in front of the chair so her feet do not touch the bare earth as she dismounts. After the bride crosses over the threshold, the groom will raise the red scarf to reveal the bride's face. Drinking wine out of the same cup completes the wedding ceremony.

Immediately after the ceremony, the couple is lead to the bridal chamber where they sit on the bed and exchange cups of honey and wine. Sometimes, for the next three days, the bedchamber is open to visitors."[10]

"In a Sudanese wedding, the ladies carry candles in a processional. There is also a showering of flowers, by dancers, to symbolize a fragrant future for the couple. An umbrella is held over the couple's head to show protection, esteem, and respect. The mother of the bride gives the bridegroom a garland of flowers, showing that he is accepted in to the family. Both the bride and groom are seated next to one another and their heads are covered with one veil indicating two people with one mind. Then a song is sung by a man and a woman, who sing a song on behalf of the parents, advising the couple to live in harmony.

The sawer is then showered on the couple that consists of rice as a sign of prosperity, coins as a sign of sharing their wealth with the less fortunate, and candy to symbolize sweetness and fragrance throughout their marriage."[11]

"In a Cherokee wedding, the bride is represented by her mother or clan mother and the oldest brother. The brother stands with her as a vow is made to take responsibility for the instructing of the children in spiritual and religious matters. This is the traditional role of the uncle.(e-du-ji). The groom's mother stands with him. A special vase is used in Cherokee marriage ceremonies and the couple drinks from the vase at the same time. The vase has two openings so that the couple can drink together.

Sometimes a blanket is used and the couple is wrapped in the blanket as a sign of their oneness. Sometimes the Cherokee start out with separate blue blankets for the bride and groom, at the beginning of the wedding, but end up with one white blanket that they share at the end. In some ceremonies, food is exchanged much the way rings are exchanged in contemporary weddings. This symbolizes that the couple will provide for one another.

The Cherokee have a sacred fire that is made with seven kinds of wood and this fire is kept burning at all times. After the sacred spot for the ceremony has been blessed seven days in a row, it is time for the ceremony of marriage. The couple would go to the scared fire in order to receive a blessing from the priest."[12]

"In Africa, weddings are a family affair. There are many ceremonies in Africa and no two are alike. In the Wolof tribe, there is a time when the elders of the village gather with the bride to give advice and gifts. Weddings in Africa can last for several days and most often involve feasting and dancing."[13]

"In Egypt, girls are married at a very young age. The night before the ceremony day, the groom and his friends will bring some of the bride price and the ceremony is preformed. The bride and groom sit face to face, with their right thumbs tied together. A reader of the Koran will tie their hands together with a handkerchief and pray for them. A few days later the couple may then live together, when the groom welcomes the bride into his home."[14]

"In Ethiopia, tattooing their abdomens with different symbols enhances the young bride's bodies."[15]

"The Masai people of Kenya give their girls, in marriage, to a man that the girl does not know and that are much older than they. At the wedding, the bride has all her belongings packed and ready to take with her to her new home. Her father spits on her head and her breasts, as a blessing, and she leaves with her husband. She never looks back for fear that she will turn to stone."[16]

"In Namibia, the bride is kidnapped before the ceremony and a leather headdress is placed on her head. Then the family anoints her with butterfat from cows, to show that they accept her."[17]

"In Pakistan, engagements only go on for one night but all the rituals and traditions associated with the wedding continue for about fifteen days. During the last two days and nights there is a celebration when the actual marriage ceremony takes place. The final ceremony happens around 3 a.m. The bride and groom are tied together and they circle a banana stalk with a bowl of burning butterfat. When the ceremony is over there is a processional to lead the bride and groom to a reception party. The procession has a drummer and around three or four dancers."[18]

Ho"ao is the Hawaiian term used for marriage which means "to stay until the dawn." The nuptials take place the eleventh night of the month.

As you can see, there are many different traditions involving courtship and marriage. There are too many to include in this book, however, we encourage you to do some research to find different ways that the people of the world begin what is, a common tradition, for most peoples of the world. The traditions are colorful, expressive, and symbolic. They are a reflection of the vast uniqueness of the creation of Yahweh.

It is clear from the scriptures that Yeshua is following the traditional Hebrew culture is His relationship to and the bridal preparation for His bride. He maintains the wedding protocol of His own culture. We lose a significant amount of beauty and meaning if we do not understand or accept the wedding protocol of our Hebrew Savior.

*And I, John, saw the set apart city, renewed Jerusalem, com -
ing down out of heaven from Elohim, prepared as a bride
adorned for her husband.* Revelation 21:2

Warfare by Honor

Chapter Eight

Grief as Honor

"It is better to go to a house of mourning than to go to
a house of feasting, for death is the destiny of every man;
the living should take this to heart." Ecclesiastes 7:2

"Blessed are those who mourn,
for they shall be be comforted." Matthew 5:4

On September 11, 2001 our country was plummeted, head long, into the grieving process. Glued to our televisions we watched, in horror, as two commercial airliners rammed into the twin towers in New York City. Thousands were killed including fire fighters, police, and emergency personnel. Hundred of people were trapped in the offices at the top of the skyscrapers, that had turned into infernos. We saw people jump from 100 story buildings to their deaths.

Warfare by Honor

During those days of non-stop television coverage, one of the things that pierced my heart was the footage of people walking the streets with pictures of their missing loved ones on posters that read *"Have you seen this person?"* The posters included descriptions of the missing loved ones.

I grimaced when I heard newscasters and politicians mention that, as Americans, we would pull ourselves up by our bootstraps and we would get back to normal. I knew that, for many Americans that had lost loved ones in the tragedy, normal, as they had known it, would never exist again.

During those days, immediately after the tragedy, I watched our country deal with their grief in a myriad of ways, due to the fact that grief is a very unique and personal experience and no one grieves in exactly the same manner.

Every people group has a protocol concerning death and grief. Even organizations like our military have a protocol concerning the honor of their dead. Soon after 9-11, I got to experience the protocol of the fire fighting community. Dennis Smith, a New York firefighter, was at ground zero helping to look for survivors, shortly after the tragedy. He describes the process of the honor given to the fallen heroes this way.

> "So now we started digging at that spot, and we find Lieutenant Warchola, from our company. I get on my cell phone and call the captain. I was off duty- I think the majority of the guys that were working there were all off duty- so the captain and all the guys who were on duty came down with the rig to get our men. This is how we do it, your company takes you out. And one by one, we take Liuetenant Warchola out, and a probie (firefighter

in training), Andy Brunn, who was one of fourteen new trainees. We found him right next to the officer. Then we pull out John Santore, Tommy Hannafin, and Louie Arena. With Chief McGovern, that made six guys from this firehouse that day. I think the greatest tribute paid to these guys is when they were carried from that eight-story pile. We had to bring them down this eighty-foot valley of bent steel and then up another, maybe four-story mountain. Then we went down again, four stories, then across the wide expanse of West Street, still deep with steel and debris, through the big entrance of the World Financial Center, and then through to the back of the Financial Center, and out to Vessey Street to where the temporary morgue is. And through the whole distance, our guys carried the chief and the men of Ladder 5 on Stokes baskets! There was an American flag over each one, and each had his helmet laying on his chest, and they were carried through a double line of firefighters, more than 300 firefighters, end to end. And as we passed, each firefighter took his helmet off and covered his heart in tribute. There was steel and concrete everywhere, and it was a tough, tough trip, a long ordeal to bring them down. But what a tribute, what a great honor to be part of it. It took five hours, and in that period that line stayed. Nobody left. These men died in that fire and that collapse, and they came down with a 5-Truck helmet on their chests. And everybody in that line was saying, "Go 5." It was the saddest day of my life and the proudest. It was also a blessing that we could bring them home to their families, bring closure to them."[1]

On this day, great honor was shown to these men by their colleagues as they painstakingly and gently carried their dead bodies, out of the make shift grave at ground zero, home to their loved ones. They gave the families a priceless gift, the gift of closure.

The value of these fallen firefighters was shown through the process of care that was taken for them. In the days that followed, the same care was shown to the family members who were now propelled into the grief process. In fact, the caring of the surviving family members by their fellow surviving firefighters was an additional form of honor shown to the dead firefighters. In caring for their families, it showed the level of commitment that the surviving firefighters felt toward their lost colleagues.

July 27th, 1999, we lost our 2-year-old granddaughter, Allie Nicole, in a drowning accident. It was a sudden, traumatic death that tore at our hearts and souls. Death is the last great battle but it is inevitable. We all must pass through its valley and shadow regardless of our status, monetary provision, intelligence, giftedness, and position in life.

When we entered this valley in 1999, I was amazed how little I had been taught in the church about death and I was equally amazed at how ill equipped the body of Christ is in dealing with this part of life that we all must pass through.

Many well-meaning believers offered quick fixes through spiritual antidotes and quoted verses from the Bible that offered little comfort. Our family was told to "Come up higher" and "Fix our minds on things above." We were told that we knew Allie was in heaven so why were we so sad. Three weeks after Allie's funeral, I was asked why we still displayed one of the funeral wreaths on our front porch. People wanted to know why we had pictures and mementos of Allie displayed in our home. Allie's mother was seven months pregnant when Allie died and a person said, " It is good she will have another baby. It will make up for Allie Nicole." Less than two months after Allie's trau-matic death, Christians warned me not to grieve too long lest we get a "spirit of grief."

> *"We have forgotten that we are but flesh and that grief itself is a form of honor."*

I could write a whole chapter of instances that happened to us that only compounded our grief and feelings of alienation from the rest of the body of Christ. It seemed that those who were able to walk closely with us and offer true comfort were others who had experienced similar losses to our own.

This lack of wisdom in the church concerning death and the grief process concerns me. It concerns me because it is dishonor. The scriptures tell us "to rejoice with those who rejoice and to weep or mourn with those who weep." It also says to "call for the wailing women" to come. There are many scriptures that speak of mourning all through the Bible and Yeshua himself wept on more than one occasion.

We have forgotten that we are but flesh and that grief itself is a form of honor.

When we grieve for someone, our grief says that that person was valuable, irreplaceable, a unique and precious gift. The deeper the loss and the more significant the person was to us, the deeper the grief we will experience. Is not a life precious to us? Can we not hesitate for a time to experience, in its fullness, the hole that is left in our lives when someone close or important to us passes from this life to the next?

My dear friend's 11-year-old daughter recently died after a 6-year battle with leukemia. Their precious little girl meant the world to them. They are strong believers in Yeshua and so is their daughter. They are assured that they will be with her in eternity. This does not keep them from missing her now. This year, their daughter's birthday was particularly difficult for my friend. When I talked to her, she shared how hard it was to go to church with the people who had been so good to walk through the illness with them, and yet not one person mentioned her daughter's birthday. She understood that they were uncomfortable and did not know what to do. We have not been taught that to remember those who have gone on before us is honor. She later told me that a young man at church came to her one day and said that he had been thinking of her daughter, and missed her so much that he drove several miles just to sit by her grave. This meant so much to my friend. This simple act of remembering her daughter was an honorable act that brought life and healing.

Dani shared a precious story to me that happened a few months after Hannah died. Dani and her family were having dinner with the family that included Hannah's best friend who I will call 'Sally.' Sally, like Hannah, was 11 years old. While gathered around the dinner table another visitor at the table asked Sally, "Who is your best friend?" Sally answered, "Hannah is my best friend." The visitor added, "But Hannah died and she is in heaven so who is your best friend now?" Sally thought for a moment and then she answered, "Hannah is still my best friend." Later Sally's mother noticed that she was missing and she went upstairs and found Sally on her bed holding a picture of Hannah. Sally said, with tears in her eyes, "Momma, I miss Hannah."

Children gift us with their heartfelt honesty and Sally was able to express what all the other adults at the table could not. To her, Hannah still existed, though in a different realm and place. Hannah was still her best friend and the loss that she felt and expressed was intense and powerful.

One of the things that we heard, when our granddaughter died, was that we would be with her again so we should get over missing her. Now I give well-meaning people this scenerio, imagine putting your child on a plane to Europe or a far away country, a place you have never visited or seen, where you will not be able to contact them by phone or mail, but knowing that when you get to heaven, your child will be there waiting for you. Then I ask them if they will miss them since they know that someday they will see them again. This is the closest I can come to explaining the powerlessness and the loneliness the loss of a loved one can bring.

In her article entitled *The Lessons of Two Tragedies* Gail Sheehy speaks about the long-term effects of the traumatic loss of loved ones in the Oklahoma bombing and at 9/11.

"Two years later support deteriorates. After a great trauma, there is a heroic phase during which friends and neighbors rise to the occasion. In the affluent suburb of Middletown, for the first six months after 9/11, people would hug and cry and talk about significant things, even with people on the street. As time passed, however, many adopted a different, popular credo for dealing with the disaster: "Time to move on." "Put it behind us." "Get over it."

Families of the Oklahoma City victims know what damage such attitudes can do. "As we passed the second anniversary, the community as a whole—families, friends, even spouses—lost patience." Recalled Richard Wintory, Oklahoma County's former senior assistant district attorney, who worked closely with the families. With the shock past and visitors thinning out, he said, "folks around the survivors didn't feel they had to cut them any slack anymore." The victims themselves wonder, 'Why can't I get passed this?'" he added. "It accelerates for some—a real downward spiral."[2]

"Grief is a type of closure that allows us to draw a line between what was, what is now, and what is to come."

We cannot get over grief, we cannot go around it and we cannot dig our way under it. We must go through it. When we refuse to allow others to naturally (and it is a natural process) grieve, we rob them and can even disable them. Unresolved grief multiplies problems and can cause physical illness, emotional sickness, and addictions.

Grief is not a sign of spiritual or emotional weakness. It is a sign that we are human beings and that we are but flesh. It is also the ultimate form of honor in that our grief shows how valuable the person that has died was and is to us. Grief is a type of closure that allows us to draw a line between what was, what is now, and what is to come. The more important the person was to us in our lives, the more impacted we will be by the loss.

I have talked to many people of faith that struggle with feelings of failure after they have lost a significant person in their lives to death. They have questioned why, if they are people of faith, can they not get over the grief quickly. They will say such things as, "I know that they are in a better place." At times these feelings of failure are exacerbated by remarks people make that reinforce this sense of failure. What we fail to remember, during these times, are the scriptures that validate the grief process and are examples of our ancestors expressing their own grief in similar life circumstances.

In Psalms 31:9 King David speaks of his own grief, "Be merciful to me, O Lord, for I am in distress; my eyes grow weak with sorrow, my soul and my body with grief."

In Psalms 13:2 again he says, "How long must I wrestle with my thoughts and every day have sorrow in my heart? How long will my enemy triumph over me?"

After King Saul and Jonathan were defeated in battle and died, 2 Samuel 1:11-12 says, "Then David and all the men with him took hold of their clothes and tore them. They mourned and wept and fasted till evening for Saul and his son Jonathan, and for the army of the Lord and the house of Israel, because they had fallen by the sword."

Paul says of his own grief in 2 Corinthians 4:8, "For out of much affliction and anguish of heart I wrote to you with many tears; not that you should be made sorrowful, but that you might know the love which I have especially for you." This verse describes the correlation between the grief that Paul had over these people and the value that he placed on his love for them.

Yeshua, also, was familiar with suffering and grief. In Isaiah 53:3 it says, "He was despised and rejected by men, a man of sorrows and familiar with suffering." Many of us know that one of the shortest verses in the bible is the verse that says,

"Yeshua wept." This verse proves that He also experienced grief and sorrow.

However, not only did He experience grief, He is moved by our grief and provides comfort for us in the grief process. Yeshua was moved by the grief of a friend in the book of John. John 11:33, "When Yeshua therefore saw her weeping, and the Jews who came with her, also weeping, He was deeply moved in spirit and was troubled."

How can it be that we, through the power of Ruach Ha Kodesh (Holy Spirit), are to be Yeshua to others and yet we cannot and will not show compassion or comfort to others. We are instructed in the scriptures as to the protocol of Yahweh concerning grief.

Yet the Lord longs to be gracious to you; He rises to show you compassion. For Adonai is an Elohim of justice. Blessed are all who wait for Him. Isaiah 30:18

Adonai is close to the brokenhearted and saves those who are crushed in spirit. Psalm 34:18

Blessed be the Elohim and Father of our Lord Jesus Christ, the Father of mercies and Yahweh of all comfort; who comforts us in all our affliction so that we may be able to comfort those who are in affliction with the comfort with which we our - selves are comforted by Yahweh." 1 Corinthians 4:3-4.

In the fall of 1998, Indigenous Christians from across the globe gathered in Rapid City, South Dakota to attend the World Christian Gathering on Indigenous Peoples. Many different tribes were there with many different cultural practices repre- sented. Every culture, however, had a ceremony that dealt with the grieving process. Our Lakota hosts gave the nations of the world an opportunity to experience their process by including them in the "wiping of the tears ceremony."

An elder explained the ceremony something like this. After a Lakota has passed away, the community and family are given a full year to experience and express the grieving process. After a year has passed, a "wiping of the tears ceremony" is held in the community. In other native cultures, a potlatch is held after the grief year has passed. In the "wiping of the tears ceremony," stories are told of the deceased, songs and prayers are made, and then an elder wipes the tears from the faces of the family and friends, signifying the grieving process, as a formal and recognized time, is over. For many family and friends, the grieving process may take years to complete but this ceremony allows the community to experience closure.

At the World Gathering, many people lined up who had experienced some type of grief and an elder came and wiped their tears with a Bible. Many experienced the presence of the Holy Spirit as Comforter during that ceremony. Many found a sense of closure to their grief and were able to face their futures with a renewed sense of hope. Then the on-lookers came and hugged the grieving ones thereby, in a sense, identifying with their grief. It was truly a time of "weeping with those who weep."

The "wiping of the tears ceremony" is a part of the Native American culture. There are other ways that the Native Americans express honor for the deceased. Some of these ways are foreign in the majority culture in America, however, we need to have respect for the ways that other cultures experience grief.

Warfare by Honor

John and Geri GrosVenor shared their experience after they attended a funeral with the Nez Perce Indians. John said,

"After the dinner, the Seven Drum Funeral service began. Geri and I entered the Longhouse (called "the home"). We went through the door in the traditional fashion; raising the right hand and turning to the left a full 360 degrees, signifying, according to some, recognition of the Scared Four Directions. Geri crossed the altar to sit in the south side, the women's side. I sat in a chair on the north side, with the men. The casket was on the altar in the center of the Longhouse. The Drummers began 7 Sacred Songs to enter the deceased person in to the "Home." The singing continued for 7 more songs. They opened the floor to anyone who wished to speak of the deceased. This time is where we may share from the heart. No reading is allowed. The floor is open to anyone to pray in spoken word or song. But, we were all cautioned not to make long speeches. But one can speak in his own language or the borrowed language of English. Then the drumming continued until midnight. The lead drummer cautions everyone not to weep aloud or permit a baby to cry for the deceased might be disturbed and be unable to find their way to the other side and she might take someone with her that night. At midnight everyone was invited to dance around the casket and "help the deceased person find their way"…and at midnight, the deceased person's spirit would turn from facing West to East and go their way, never to recognize any of us until we crossed over to "the other side." After the midnight ceremony, dinner again was served. Seven more songs would be sung at 5:00 a.m. and then the body would be buried at 6:00 a.m." We do not believe everything taught by the Seven Drum people. There are many teachings that we cannot accept. But, there are also many songs sung to the Creator and there are teachings, which we do wholeheartedly accept that conform in principle and spirit to Scripture."[3]

John and Geri may not have agreed with every custom and expression of the Nez Perce but they still showed themselves to be people of honor in a good way in their dealings with these people. We can all learn a lesson from the GrosVenors. We can learn to respect the differences in people and allow others to grieve in their own unique ways. We can support them through this process by doing as the GrosVenors, simply being present in the grief of those around us. The simple act of showing up emotionally and physically for others during this time is so important.

"In December 1890, a few hours after Chief Sitting Bull's assassination, Chief Big Foot attempted to lead 350 Lakota women, children and elderly 300 miles across South Dakota. Federal soldiers trapped these people on a field called Wounded Knee and killed every man, woman and child. What followed was a century of humiliation and poverty as the Lakota were forced on to reservations. In 1986 a small group of Lakota decided to acknowledge their collective losses through an act that would bring honor to their ancestors and those who perished at Wounded Knee.

From 1986 to 1990 the Lakota participated in an event called the Chief Big Foot Memorial Ride. The event would involve a horse back ride from Sitting Bull's assassination site to Wounded Knee. The event would culminate on December 29, 1990 on the 100th anniversary of the Wounded Knee massacre with a "Wiping Away of Tears" ceremony. Although the original vision was completed in 1990, the Lakota elders decided to give permission for the ride to become an annual event. It was renamed Future Generations Riders and the riders are now mostly children. The event has actually become a "coming of age" event."[4]

This event helps the children to accept who they are as Lakota by acknowledging what their ancestors have endured. They are also allowed to grieve the losses that affected all Lakota at Wounded Knee. Many of the children have pledged to return annually in a commitment sealed as they purify themselves in a sweat lodge. The children are taught that they are honoring the memory of their deceased ancestors who died at Wounded Knee as they make this ride for them.

One of the things that this ceremony has provided for the Lakota people is closure. Closure is so important and we, as Americans, have not been trained in the importance of it or how to proceed in gaining it.

Several years ago a friend of mine named Barbara and her husband Doug had a miscarriage. They had wanted this baby so badly and it was quite a shock to them when they lost the baby. Many of the people from our church were with them at the hospital during the birth process of the baby. Barbara came home from the hospital without her beloved child and everyone seemed to get back to business as usual. I noticed that we as believers seemed to have no process of closure for those families who miscarry. It seemed strange to me since the conservative part of the church is so adamant on the value of life. The message given through the lack of closure for the families of miscarriage seemed to be "We value life as long as it is living here and we can see it and as long as that life produces."

Days went by and I could not shake the uneasy feeling that I had about leaving Doug and Barbara comfortless. As I began to pray for and about them, I was directed by the Holy Spirit to ask their permission to have a memorial service for their baby that we would host and they could attend should they desire. I did not want them to feel responsible to do anything or to perform for any one.

They were touched that we would want to remember their child and were more than willing to attend. We began the service by affirming our belief that their son was with Yeshua and the Father in heaven. We read scriptures that confirmed this belief. We had different people share from their hearts concerning Doug, Barbara and their child. Our worship dance team then did a dance to a song called "A Visitor From Heaven" that is about a child who dies and the blessing that the life of the child had brought to the world. We finished the service by surrounding Doug and Barbara in the middle of our circle and by praying prayers of encouragement for them. When the service was over Doug and Barbara expressed the gift that this ceremony had been to them. It not only lessened the burden of heaviness but it eliminated the isolation that many experience when they walk through grief. The powerful lesson for me was that the service not only helped Doug and Barbara but it profoundly helped all of us who were their friends and colleagues. We no longer were afraid to speak of the child or of what to say. This act of allowing and expressing grief had broken down barriers and walls for all of us. It was an intimate time that we will never forget.

When I was a therapist, I would encourage my clients, who were stuck in the process of unresolved grief, to acknowledge their grief by taking account of the losses in their lives. Some had loved ones that they had lost to death and had left many things unsaid. I encouraged those individuals to write a letter to their loved one in which they would bare their souls with transparent honesty. I then instructed them, if at all possible, to make a trip to the graveside of their loved one where they would read their letter and then bury it. Many times this would bring closure to people and allow them to move on and embrace life. What follows is another example of how one woman's grief propells her to help others who are involved in the grief process.

"In 1993, Tina Zarlenga's five year old son suddenly passed away. She wanted to keep his memory alive so she created memory sheets, which included a series of questions that asked family and friends about her son. The outpouring she received, even from people that she did not know, overwhelmed her. Five years later, in 1998, her father passed away and once again she passed out the memory sheets and gathered memory books for her whole family about her father. As a result, Tina and her family realized that more needed to be done to help grieving families. The grief that they experienced taught this family that the first year after the loss of a loved one is a crucial time. Family members can feel left behind as others go on with their lives and do not realize the hole left in the hearts of the bereaved family.

Out of Tina's loss and pain came the company IMO—In Memory Of. With the aid of family and friends, IMO creates and delivers a personalized monthly greeting, which celebrates the life of the deceased person. Monthly tributes consist of stories, photos, and dedications submitted by family and friends. In addition, the service includes educational tips and suggestions on how to support the bereaved family. Memories are one of the greatest gifts that one can give a bereaved person."[5]

The first year after Allie died, we joined other families that had lost their children to death by gathering at a Christmas service where the pictures of the children were flashed across a large screen and families were called up to light a candle in honor of the deceased child. Although painful, what a comfort to be able to do something, though small, to honor Allie and to say to the world, "She was, is and always will be important to us. Let us never forget that she was here and made a permanent impact on our lives."

The first Christmas after my father died, I made framed picture collages of each of my family members with my dad. We gathered in the family room on Christmas Eve and as I presented each of them with the pictures. I lit a candle that I had given them with their gifts. As I went around the circle and lit the candles the room was illuminated with light. I concluded with a song that was special to my father and lit a single candle, in the middle of the circle, in honor of him. We all cried and it was a difficult time to share but it was healing to us all. The lighted candles reminded us, that as a family united, we sent forth a greater light that would continue to shine within the darkness of the darkest nights of our souls. My father's candle reminded us that my father was still with us and that his candle still burned across the veil that we would one day pass through.

It has been five years since Allie died and almost two since Hannah died. Both girls' birthdays are in June. This year Kimberly (Allie's mother), Dani (Hannah's mother), our mutual friend Debbie, and myself gathered at a local restaurant to share a time of fellowship. As we caught up on events of one another's lives, Dani shared with us that it was Hannah's birthday. It just so happened that in three days it would be Allie's birthday as well. After our lunch we ordered a birthday cake, and we cried as we each told what these girls had meant and continued to mean to us as mothers, grandmothers, and friends. We then sang happy birthday to them and ate our cake through tears of sorrow and joy. We spoke of how we missed the girls and how we would not trade anything in our lives to have known them, and we spoke of how we longed to see their sweet faces again. It was an honorable time. Was it difficult? Yes, it was difficult but it was oh so rich! Those girls are worthy of celebrating their births. Just because they are not here with us in body does not mean that they no longer exist in our hearts, minds, or in the presence of Yahweh.

Grief as Honor

Why, if these times of expression of grief are so rewarding and rich, do we avoid them? We avoid them because grief brings us into an awkward place with people. We hate to see others suffer, and do not want to believe that we too might suffer in the same or even greater ways in our own unknown futures. It is so much easier to walk away and pretend not to notice the unfairness in life that death can bring.

What are we to do? Here are some suggestions that might help if you are walking along side someone in the valley of the shadow of death.

1. People in grief DO NOT need lectures. Please do not scold or preach.

2. Remain calm and non-judgmental.

3. Encourage them to talk and allow them to tell their story to you over and over.

4. Mention the deceased by name.

5. Let them cry for as loud and as long as they need.

6. Do not make them feel rushed through the process.

7. If they want to talk about the loss, do not make them feel that they are negative and do not try to change the subject to a "lighter" topic.

8. Do not say that you know how they feel. Grief is unique.

9. If they want to be silent that is ok. Take your cues from them.

10. Do not tell them how good they look to avoid talking about their pain.

11. Be available to listen, especially in the evenings.

12. Do not be afraid to gently hug or touch them but ask them first. Some people are uncomfortable with touch.

13. Help them with practical matters in life; watching children, grocery shopping, making meals, house cleaning, and running errands until they can enter back in to life.

14. Make several short visits.

15. Send cards.

16. Ask if they need financial help.

17. Show your own frailties so that they do not feel like the mission field.

18. Minister to the whole family but do not allow them to form an unhealthy dependency on you.[6]

Although it is painful, expressing grief is a part of embracing reality. Grief cannot be rushed and it does not follow a direct route. Unlike the saying "time heals all wounds," time alone will not heal grief. Work is required in order to get through the grieving process. Grief is hard work but it is good work. Embracing grief is an honorable thing to do.

There are steps that we can take to embrace our grief and in so doing honor our loved one.

1. Acknowledge our grief and take the time to understand it

2. Write a loss history that identify the losses through your life and how intense they were and are, make a collage to help you express how you feel or use colors to describe your feelings.

3. Allow your grief needs to be recognized by others (be transparent and humble).

4. Feel free to grieve in your own unique way without feeling "less than" or "weird."

5. Tell others your story and honestly account the loss.

6. Learn life's lessons thorough the experience and become more compassionate.

7. Commit to choosing life by embracing the grief journey, however long it takes.

8. Share the comfort and wisdom you have received with others.

9. Trust Yahweh and cling to Him. Always be honest with Him about your feelings. He is Yahweh, He can handle it.[7]

The Scriptures teach us that Yeshua "will not put out a smoldering wick and will not break a bruised reed." He is not afraid to comfort the broken hearted and those who are crushed in spirit. If we have His Holy Spirit within us then we should not be afraid to embrace the suffering of others. Yahweh has never been afraid of broken-ness. Out of broken-ness He healed hearts, healed bodies, distributed food, restored hope, rebuked hypocrisy, and redeemed the world. Sometimes the "broken-ness" of people's lives is manifested by divorce, bankruptcy, illness, addiction, and depression, all of which include some level and form of grieving. Yahweh is not "put off" by these true to life situations and neither should we. We, however, must learn to not be afraid of broken-ness. This fear can be overcome.

As ambassadors in His kingdom, we are to be agents of His protocol concerning grief. He makes it clear that we are to "bring good news to the afflicted, to bind up the broken-hearted, to proclaim liberty to captives and freedom to prisoners and to comfort those who mourn (see Luke 4:18)."

"What an honor it is to be used as an agent of healing in the lives of others!"

If we are obedient to this task, we will bring the oil of gladness and a mantle of praise. We will be called "oaks of righteousness," and we will be co-builders with Him of ancient ruins and former devastations. We will repair the ruined places and desolations of many generations.

What an honor it is to be used as an agent of healing in the lives of others! Can we take the time to be that in the earth? Can we trust the hearts of those we love to the Creator, and give Him the time He needs to allow true healing to come to these beloved people? Can we absorb their pain without trying to "fix it" for them and, secretly, for ourselves?

When Allie died, we missed her face, her smell, her smile, and her touch. We ached for her because holding and interacting with our other grandchildren could not take the place of Allie. She was and is and will always be irreplaceable. The Creator made each of us to be a one-of-a-kind gift. To refuse to acknowledge that, by refusing to grieve the losses of the people in our lives, is to deal with the gift of life in a way that is not sacred and is, actually, dishonorable.

I am aware of the passion that Christians display when confronted with the issue of abortion. Many are quick to quote scriptures that prove the value of a life and that each life is a precious gift from God. This is so true. What confuses me is the inconsistency of how we walk out this belief. If we really believe that each life is a unique and precious gift, then why do we discourage others from feeling the loss of these gifts deeply and authentically? When we make light of our grief and the grief of others, concerning the loss of a loved one, aren't we, in essence, saying that this person was not that important in life?

Can we allow ourselves to stop for a time and honor the memory of the one we have lost to death? Can we honor Yahweh by taking the time to reflect on the blessing of His creation in this person that He has given to us? We can, if we will humble ourselves and be willing to enter the shadow lands as agents of mercy.

Bear one another's burdens, and thus fulfill the law of Christ. Galatians 6:2

Warfare by Honor

Chapter Nine

Entering Another Nation

"Our culture is once again thriving. Many ceremonies are being revived with the young taking an active part along with the elders....a new culture has evolved, a culture which has blended remnants of the past with adoptions from a new way of life."[1]

Pat Deiter McArthur, Plains Cree Nation

"Thieves and robbers come over the wall but true shepherds come through the gatekeeper, and the gatekeeper opens the gate for them." Yeshua (John 10:1-3)

"They made us many promises, more than I can remember. But they kept but one—they promised to take our land... and they took it." Chief Red Cloud

Warfare by Honor

In our book *Can You Feel the Mountains Tremble? A Healing the Land Handbook*, we write about gatekeepers and gatekeeping. "Gatekeeping is simply establishing a spiritual immigration policy. Every piece of ground or territory has an entrance and exit place on it. Such places are called the gates of that territory. Every gate has a gatekeeper."[2]

Let's assume that what the Scriptures say in Acts 17:26 is true: that "the Creator made all the nations from one man. The Creator established the boundaries and borders of all the nations. The Creator established the seasons of their stewardship over the lands where He placed them." Therefore the chief or leader over a tribe or nation is the *gatekeeper* of that nation.

When someone entered a nation not his own, he/she would first meet with the Chief and receive permission to travel, camp, hunt, or trade within that nation. The protocol of meeting with a chief would include a formal presentation of the traveler's name, the purpose of the journey, the length of stay, etc. Gifts and honors would be exchanged, and permission would be granted or withheld by the gatekeeper. "With permission the immigrant possessed a new measure of authority, not 'taken' but 'gifted,' to proceed to the desired destination."[3]

Sadly, this is not what happened on the shores of North America when the immigrants entered the land, and it is not what happened for most of the indigenous peoples of the world. The protocol of honor was breached and not only have the host people suffered, the offspring of the immigrants have suffered as well. The host people were robbed of the honor of being the stewards of this continent and the immigrants were robbed of an honorable welcome on to the land.

Let us share a scripture that Yahweh has enlightened to us. The scripture we are speaking of is about Queen Jezebel. When Jezebel is used as a teaching tool in the church, she is often used as a bad role model for women. Women are cautioned, "Don't be a Jezebel." And sometimes this means, "don't be a strong and powerful woman." I don't think I have ever heard the scriptures on Jezebel taught in the way that Yahweh revealed it to us.

*And it came to be, after these events, that Naboth, the Jezreelite, had a vineyard which was in Jezreel near the palace of Ahab, the King of Samaria. So Ahab Spoke to Naboth saying, "Give me your vineyard, that I may have it for a vegetable garden, because it is near, next to my house; and for it I will give you a vineyard better than it. Or, if it seems good to you, I will give you it's worth in money." And Naboth said to Ahab, "The Lord forbid that I should give the **inheritance** of my fathers to you!" So Ahab went in to his house, sullen and displeased because of the word which Naboth, the Jezreelite had spoken to him; for he had said, "I will not give you the inheritance of my fathers." (see 1 Kings 22)*

In these scriptures Jezebel tells her husband that she will get the vineyard for Ahab and she cooks up a scheme in which to have Naboth killed so that her husband, the King can have the land.

So it was, when Ahab heard that Naboth was dead, that Ahab got up and went down to take possession of the vineyard of Naboth the Jezereelite (see I Kings 22:2-16).

Warfare by Honor

Here we have the deeper revelation of the spirit of Jezebel. It is about **stealing inheritance**. Notice that Naboth said, "I can not give you the **inheritance** of my fathers." This means that it was also Naboth's inheritance and the inheritance that Naboth would leave to his children or heirs. Jezebel killed in order to take land and in so doing stole the inheritance of Naboth's family. The spirit of Jezebel is alive in North America, resonant on the land. We can just as easily substitute the name "First Nation's of North America" in place of Naboth because the intent and the outcome was the same. I guess that explains why we have difficulty overcoming that spirit in our lives and churches. Our homes and churches are built on land defiled by this spirit. We are trying to prosper in "Naboth's vineyard" and it was acquired in an unholy, unrighteous transaction.

The only way that we can combat this spirit is by acting in the opposite spirit. Jezebel and Ahab acted dishonorably and unjustly in dealing with Naboth. Historically, our country and our churches have acted dishonorably and unjustly in our dealings with the native peoples. The opposite of dishonor is purposeful honor, and we demonstrate that through radical humility.

People ask us all the time, "What can I do to show honor to people of other cultures or denominations?" We can share with you a story that we pray will challenge your paradigms and stir your heart to action.

I, (Suuqiina) was invited to speak at an Alaskan village of a tribe other than my own. We were of different cultures, stewards of different territories. I sought an audience with their Grand-Chief and one was granted to me.

I was ushered into the chief's home and presented before him. He asked me, "What is your name?" I answered by giving him my mother's name, my grandmother's name, and identified my great-grandfather as chief of a village.[4] He asked, "What is your mission amongst our people?" I replied by identifying my work amongst First Nations people. He responded by blessing me with a personal prayer, welcoming me onto the land, and declaring protection for me amongst his people. What a powerful blessing was extended to me and to the ultimate success of my work amongst his nation. I asked him how many workers had presented themselves to him for a welcome and blessing. His answer, both discouraging and disturbing, was very few.

"Note that most often people with authority don't have to tell anyone. They simply wear it like a mantel."

Yeshua called people who "climb over walls" "thieves and robbers." Why? It is because they steal the honor and dignity of the chief. They usurp authority by "taking" it rather than being "gifted" by someone who has the authority. Note that most often people with authority don't have to tell anyone. They simply wear it like a mantel.

Honoring a chief, a gatekeeper, requires one to become humble. Following protocol is one expression of that humility. If walls have been scaled and gatekeepers ignored, it is never too late to return with humility, repentance and seek the gift of a "do over."

In 1999 it was my privilege to visit Israel for the first time. I joined a group of 96 First Nations people from North America for the Feast of Tabernacles. Our group leader was Grand-Chief Linda Prince, Carrier-Sekani of Canada. She had arranged a protocol meeting with President Avrim Berg, leader of the Knesset, the legislative house of Israel's democracy. We consider President Berg to be the "gatekeeper" of Israel as one of the Heads of State.

We were given just fifteen minutes to protocol the President with our gifts. Before we were to close with an honor song, Grand-Chief Prince stood and said, "What a privilege to be with the first of all the first nations of the world. We have lost control of our governments as First Nations of North America. We have lost most of our land. We do not control what our nations do or how we are represented. However, we are still stewards of the land. We are responsible before the Creator for what happens on our land. Therefore, we repent and take responsibility for the incident of the St. Louis.[5] We ask forgiveness for the tragic and horrible things that your people experienced by this event."

This was an unforeseen act of humility done by Grand-Chief Prince on behalf of Canada and the United States. President Berg called his secretary over and cancelled the remainder of his schedule for that day and spent another hour and forty-five minutes with us. He shared about the relationship between North America and Israel. He spoke of how the Israelis admired the natives of North America. At one point he asked someone to tell him how we had come to faith. Chief Will Mayo, Alaskan Athabascan, gave his personal testimony of coming to faith in Yeshua. History was being made that day in Israel.

As our time with President Berg came to a close, we sang an honor song which is a repetitive chant using the name

Yahweh. As Israeli television broadcast this event live, President Berg joined us at the drum wearing an ancient headdress gifted to him. After the song, he said, "I know you believe in most if not all of the New Testament, but I give you authority to do what you came here to do and I offer you my personal protection." He then raised his hands and cited in Hebrew, "Blessed is he who comes in the name of the Lord." It was a time when our tears flowed freely and our hearts were moved beyond belief.

During our time in Israel, we were honored everywhere we went. People talked with us. They wanted to meet and greet us. They wanted to touch us when we wore our regalia. They opened their hearts to us simply because we had come through the gatekeeper and he had opened the gate for us.

We went to the Western Wall to pray, joining people from all over the world. We wore full regalia, what we like to call our priestly garments. We could hear people calling on their cell phones, "Come down here, the Indians are here and they are worshipping our God." We were mobbed in a good way. In fact a group of soldiers came and escorted out of the area for our own safety. (It is sad to say but we are loved in every country of the world but one—our own.)

President Berg gave the First Nations of North America a standing invitation to visit the Knesset every year and receive his blessing upon our stay in Israel.

What price could be put on the power of Protocol? What gates could we have opened for ourselves compared to the gate opened for us? Can you imagine the authority given to us that would never compare to the authority we could have stolen?

Thousands of believers make a pilgrimage to Israel every year. Sad to say but very few ever go through the gatekeeper. Very few even contact the local messianic leaders and become aware of the messianic influence in Israel. Most simply tramp all over Israel making proclamations, declaring promises, "walking where Yeshua walked," singing songs of worship, praying prayers of blessing, and claiming an inheritance without consideration of their "older brother," and the fact that as believers, they are rooted into Israel, not the other way around. Remember Judaism doesn't need Christianity to explain its existence but Christianity requires Judaism to explain its existence.

"Protocol is the voice of honor."

"Every man must treat with respect all such things as are sacred to other people, whether he comprehends them or not." [6]

It may be impossible to understand every aspect of what protocol does, how it honors, why it works, and the depth of feeling it conveys, but it is possible to learn about it and practice it when information about a culture is available to you.

Like hope, joy, fear, intimidation, affirmation, and all such "feeling" aspects of life, honor cannot be considered an exact science but it can convey a feeling for those honored which can never be denied or overlooked. Very few people in our world will reject honor that is presented as genuine and heartfelt. Protocol carries the weight of the honor that is being bestowed. Protocol is the voice of honor.

There is a proper and honorable way to enter a land not one's own. We seldom give thought to this way unless we are world travelers who might experience the complications of entering and departing some nations of the world.

Because of a history of *manifest destiny*, most Euro-Americans have an understanding that says they have a right to go anywhere, anytime, unhindered, and settle anywhere without opposition. This so-called *manifest destiny* was and is a lie that has been used to create unspeakable hardships for indigenous people everywhere and to dishonor them in the most egregious ways possible.

Most immigrant people have never gifted the indigenous leader(s) of the lands where they reside. Most religious organizations haven't been welcomed, formally, onto the land by the indigenous people of the land. Most chiefs have never been visited or gifted by those visiting or settling on their lands. Many immigrants haven't studied the culture of the indigenous host people of the lands where they reside. Most have not entered the land with proper protocol and everyone suffers for it.

"And so I say to you, the EuroCanadians; you have discovered our land and its resources, but you have not yet discovered my people nor our teachings, nor the spiritual basis of our teachings." (Chief John Snow, Wesley Band, Stoney Nation)[7]

The third World Christian Gathering on Indigenous People was held at Meroo, Australia in 2000. Indigenous people from 31 nations of the world gathered to worship, pray, sing, dance, and share their cultures. One of the speakers was John Dawson, Founder of the Reconciliation Coalition who spoke on *The Place of Immigrant Peoples*. Here are some excerpts from that timely and challenging message.

"I am a pakeha person—a white—at a conference that is for indigenous people. My purpose in coming here was not to teach...It is a surprise...a privilege to be invited because people like me don't deserve to be here because of the story of these nations. There has been great grace extended toward us...

We are arrogant to you because we have a deep-seated belief in our own superiority. Even when our intellect and our theology rejects that idea, the fact is that our eyes and our posture and our tone of voice—our body language—still betray us. It's not the truth about everybody, but it's a general truth. It is certainly the truth about me. Sometimes we are most arrogant when we think we're being the most kind.

If you had told me I was arrogant towards these people, I would have been very hurt and said, 'Look, I love these people' and that is true. There is such a depth of deception in our culture—a deep-seated belief in our superiority. It's a prison of pride.

The second reason we wound and hurt you is that we have massive unresolved corporate guilt over the past. Whenever we see your black or brown faces walking toward us—at an unconscious level, it reminds us of our shame. There are two ways of dealing with shame: to blame and degrade the people who make us feel bad, or to deal with it at the foot of the cross and openly confess it before the people we have offended.

I come to you as an adopted member of the New Zealand Aotearoa continent—adopted into the Maori family by Sam. I began to ask this question: Is there a way to righteously gain a place in someone else's inheritance?

There are some basic principles.

The world is God's. 'The earth is the Lords and the fullness thereof,' I often chant and dance this out— sometimes in a North American way and sometimes as a Maori haka, approaching the powers of darkness and declaring this truth.

There is also a Psalm (115:16) that says 'The heavens are the Lord's but He has given the earth to mankind.' So the world consists of a series of jurisdictions or inheritances....Do we qualify to inherit anything that is God's? That is the question.

There are two spirits in which you can enter somebody else's jurisdiction: righteous or unrighteous. Abraham and Ruth are our positive models. Abraham was entering Canaan, and Ruth was entering Israel. Both Ruth and Abraham represent the pilgrim settler.

The negative spirit would be the colonizer with an imperialist spirit.

1. The colonizer with an imperialist spirit, if given voice would sound something like this, (an exaggerated statement for the sake of illustration):

You will yield to the will of our leader expressed through me—yield to our superior culture, which is better qualified to exercise jurisdiction. Decision has already been made concerning our common future, we will apportion any resources that may

be discovered in the land. We will decide if any of
your culture is worthy of being retained. Our cultural identity must not be compromised by
dwelling in this, our new territory. Your women
will provide comfort, but children that may result
will not be given inclusion among us.

This is proclamation of authority, a jurisdictional
claim upon territory, the extension of authority by use
of implements of power, the extraction of wealth for
the singular benefit of a home culture.

That is one extreme which cannot be justified in
the Word of God....and when I look at that I tremble
before God because of the degree to which we came in
that spirit.

Abraham shows a legitimate place for people find-
ing hope and new beginnings in a new land.

2. **The Pilgrim Settler** might come speaking like this:

May I dwell among your people as an adopted child,
sharing in your inheritance. You have the right of
refusal. I will honor and serve you with my gifts and
culture. I acknowledge my need of your gifts and
culture. We could seek mutual benefit by adjusting
laws and custom to the needs of our common
wealth. May our sons and daughters be free to find
each other in marriage and thus create a new people through our union. Recognizing that all inheritances are given by God, I will covenant with you to
discover the purpose of God for the inhabitants of
this region as we serve other peoples from other

regions, but I recognize that the greater honor is to be given to your culture in perpetuity, because God has placed you here before us.

Note: The term culture is used here to denote the art, per - sonality and protocol of a people, which is morally neutral.

What does the Bible teach about how we qualify to inherit a place? In Genesis 12, God says to Abraham to come out from among your own people and go to another place. To come out also means to go in. If you come out from somewhere, you go into somewhere else—and usually there is an indigenous people there.

Abraham was like Captain Cook wandering around in transit. He's passing through and he comes up to that place that later is to be called Jerusalem, and he finds one of the host people of the land who is a religious guy—a priest—whose name is Melchizedek. This guy is worshipping God but he's not using the name Yahweh or any name Abraham is familiar with. He is using the name El Elyon. He dresses weird, he speaks funny. He uses a different language, and he's worshipping a god that Abraham has never heard of. He is identified in the Bible as a Jebusite. But Abraham is just beginning to understand himself, so he's not arrogant. It took meekness and humility to understand that this guy was actually worshipping the Most High.

1. He began to honor the indigenous people of the land in their knowledge of God—HUMILITY;

2. Participate in ethical actions—JUSTICE;

3.Take responsibility for priestly mediation—MERCY.

This lines up with Micah 6:8 'He has shown you, O man, what is good. And what and what does the Lord require of you? To act justly and to love mercy and to walk humbly with your God.'

Let me explain these three things from the life of Abraham. Firstly, as Abraham came to Melchizedek, he bowed down and he tithed to him. By tithing to this guy, Abraham was recognizing not only that he was in someone else's jurisdiction, but also that he was a priest of the Most High God. A radical sense of honor is being given there.

Secondly, we see Abraham became involved in ethical actions. He became concerned for the justice issues in the land. His nephew, Lot, was living among the people of Sodom. They were invaded, dispossessed and carried away into captivity. Abraham didn't just go after Lot in a commando raid. He rescued all the people of Sodom. They risked their lives to restore this people group to their inheritance, and wouldn't take any payment for it. That is an ethical action.

Thirdly, God comes to Abraham over the same group of people to say 'I'm going to judge Sodom.' Why does God tell him this? Because God is always looking for an intercessor. So he (Abraham) begins to stand in the gap and pleads for the city. Abraham lived out these principles almost a thousand years before David entered the city of Jerusalem.

How do we qualify to inherit the land? It is a courtship in which God is the third party, like a young man who approaches someone's father to ask for her hand in marriage. God is watching us. The biggest problem that we have is offending the Lord by not looking at the values of scripture, assuming our superiority, asserting jurisdiction in the name of Jesus in a satanic way—an imperialistic, controlling, arrogant way. This misrepresents the character of God.

The process (protocol) of gaining relationship with one another should be: proximity, observation, attraction, courtship, covenant, intimacy, fruitfulness, celebration."[8]

"Protocol has this wonderful way of putting in a proper place, deserved honor, where we are not diminished by honoring others."

John Dawson has expressed, in his gifted manner, some of the principles involved in properly entering another's land. There is a way, an honorable way, to enter every piece of land upon the earth. This way is often easier found than the humility to seek it in the first place. Protocol has this wonderful way of putting in a proper place, deserved honor, where we are not diminished by honoring others. All parties retain honor in the protocol ceremony. Again, and it can't be stressed deeply enough, this honor must come from the heart. It must be genuine in order to have integrity.

It seems (see Rev. 5-8) that a cosmic protocol will be observed when entering heaven. This protocol includes pageantry, procession of the nations with the inclusion of their respective cultures (ie. languages, regalia, dances, etc.), and the heavenly hosts with Yeshua Himself orchestrating the whole ceremony. It seems we will not simply saunter into heaven greeting everyone with "high-fives." Protocol will be observed for the benefit of all entering and for their extravagant blessing.

Protocol can be observed if someone moves to a new community, city, state, or country. Arrangements can be made to see the Chief, Mayor, Council, Governor, and even the Head of the Country and present a gift and receive a welcome to the land. These efforts will always be rewarded with a newly acquired sense of dignity, honor, and even authority. Hawaiians have a word for doing what's right—it's called "pono." There is power in doing what is right and being right with those where one lives.

If you happen to be the person with the authority (ie. a chief or a mayor), prepare to receive honor and graciously extend a welcome, a blessing, and gift authority to those who may show honor through protocol.

Learning to give honor where it's due and to receive honor when appropriate is all part of the proper way of entering another's land.

We always make a point of asking for a welcome and a blessing in our travels. When we are invited into an area to teach a seminar, it is our custom to meet with the indigenous people and their leader(s) of that area.

When we moved to Tennessee, we traveled to Cherokee, North Carolina to meet with the Cherokee Chief and ask for his blessing to reside on the land. We shared with him our belief that:

1. The Creator has given the Cherokee people stewardship over the land by sovereignly placing them in the southeast (see Acts 17:26-27).

2. The gifts and callings (stewardships) of Yahweh are irrevocable (see Romans 11:29).

3. The Cherokee continue to retain stewardship over all original Cherokee land although they have been removed to a smaller reservation by the immigrants.

The Chief graciously welcomed us to the Tennessee area, said he hoped we would live in peace and prosper there, and he gave us authority to teach our message "in all land that was ever Cherokee land."

We also made a trip to the mayor of our city. When we met with him, we shared the same scriptures and stated that we believe that Yahweh places people in authority. We wanted to respect his authority and be a blessing to him and our community. We gave him a gift. He was overwhelmed in a good way. He said, "No one has ever come by here and gifted me for doing my job. I thought you had come here to complain. Could you get more people like you to move to our city? I need more people that have your attitude."

The scriptures say "A man's gifts make room for him." Jacob used this wisdom when he was reentering the land of his brother Esau. He had cheated Esau out of his birthright, his inheritance. Jacob sent out groups of servants bearing gifts for Esau to show his humility to his offended brother. Jacob knew that when entering the land of another's, protocol must be followed in order to keep peace and receive a welcome.

Yeshua was part of one such welcoming ceremony in Matthew 21. This is commonly known as the Triumphal Entry and it is celebrated on Palm Sunday. Most of us never realized we were commemorating a protocol ceremony. Yeshua was a resident of Nazareth in Galilee and was now being welcomed into Jerusalem. This was proper protocol for a person of influ-ence and authority.

In the United States of America we send ambassadors to many countries. Their chief role is to keep good relationships between our country and the country where they are sent. Every ambassador has a full-time protocol officer who is responsible to know the customs and culture of that country. Their job is to keep offences to a minimum.

It only makes sense that believers in Yeshua, as ambassa-dors of the gospel, would operate with the same wisdom and caution that the world uses in dealing with domestic and glob-al affairs. We represent a King and His kingdom. He has com-missioned us to travel the earth bringing to others the great-est protocol gift ever given. What a shame if we go in a dis-honorable way, offending people, and preventing the message from being heard. We must become people of honor. We have the time to do it right the first time. We may not be awarded the opportunity to do it over. Let us learn protocol and in so doing...be wise.

Chapter Ten

Cross Cultural Awareness

Time alone has not heightened cultural awareness.
Norine Dresser, *Multicultural Manners*

How does someone begin understanding mixing people with different backgrounds, perceptions of reality, manners, habits and beliefs? It all begins with cross-cultural awareness. It is developing a greater understanding of the widely differing cultures and sensibilities of each country in which participants do business, ministry, or even visits.

Here is an example from the Windham International Cultural Model© one or two day programs for expatriates and their spouses/familes:

"**Background information: History, politics, and events.** Discussions about history, politics, religion, and current events help put the country and culture in perspective and define the historic relationship with the hone country.

Daily living. A recently repatriated individual shares information about living in the new country. We select resource people who can discuss relevant information about shopping, schools, health care, recreation, social activities, customs, and other family interests and concerns. They also discuss and provide information about the expatriate community in the new location.

Business Issues. Conducting business in the destination culture is discussed by an outside resource person who has worked in the host and destination cultures. We try to assure that the resource person held a similar position in the same or related industry, and in other ways matches the profile of the participant. Our staff carefully selects and prepares the resource person, and the counselor conducting the program keeps it focused and responsive to the expatriate's needs and interests.

Cultural framework. The Windham International Cultural Model© is used to teach the expatriate and spouse/family the similarities and differences between the host and destination cultures. Each expatriate completes an assessment of his or her own personal characteristics using the Model. This allows them to see the differences and bridge the cultural gap between their personal scores on the Model and the characteristics they will encounter in the destination culture. Together with the counselor, they create strategies to help them bridge the cultural gap. The Cultural Model© introduces them to nine cultural dimensions, which they have an opportunity to discuss. The cultural dimensions include hierarchy, change tolerance, group dependence, diversity receptivity, status attainment, relationships, communication, time, and space.

Personal cultural profile. We identify the unique cultural profile of the employees and spouses/families and their innate cultural biases which will play a role in their cultural adjustment in the destination culture.

Family issues and the culture shock cycle. The culture chock cycle is explained, and participants review suggestions for addressing cultural differences. Other concerns that are addressed include raising children in another culture and keeping in touch with family and friends back home."

Windham is only one of many programs and protocol schools being offered around the world. While such preparations may seem complex and may even be expensive, they may save your job, your integrity, or even your life.

Here is an example from the Cross Cultural Journeys Foundation and their travel philosophy.

"As responsible travelers we:

Travel in a spirit of humility and with a genuine desire to meet and talk with local people.

Are aware of the feelings of the locals and respect their customs in our actions.

Always respect temples and other sacred places and their holy artifacts as we would the churches and temples in our homelands.

Show particular respect when we photograph: exchange a few words and then ask permission to photograph; respect a "no."

Cultivate the habit of being present, of listening, of not always talking and having answers, of learning by watching.

Realize that other people may have concepts of time and thought patterns different from ours—not inferior, just different.

Discover the richness of everyday activities in another culture instead of always seeking the exotic.

Remember that we are among many visitors, and do not expect special privileges.

Make no promises to local people that we cannot implement; keep the promises that we make.

Spend time each day reflecting on our experiences, considering the possibility that what enriched us may have robbed another."

Consider, for a moment, how different history might be told if these simple travel philosophies had been adhered to by all global travelers? Its almost mind boggling to consider. The lack of protocol has wreaked havoc upon our world simply because of arrogance and ignorance.

We found an international protocol certification program that costs about $7500 per person for a one week program. Is this cost too high? Maybe it is an investment and not a cost when dignity, integrity, success, honor, and our futures are at stake.

Protocol Consultants International says, "We are now immersed in the most competitive business climate in history and are engaged in a global economy which has created significant competitive pressures on managers and executives at all levels of the organization. Technology, book and business knowledge aside, it's still all about PEOPLE, and interacting with people. It is your behavior from the onset which will help foster a positive rapport with employers, business associates and clients.

"Knowledge is power. Protocol empowers."

Knowledge is power. Protocol empowers. Knowledge of protocol empowers confidence and authority to out class the competition. Being mindful of others is key to effective social and business relationships."

John D. Rockerfeller said, "I will pay more for the ability to deal with people than for any other ability under the sun."

The programs and quotes listed in this chapter were all from presentations and web pages on the internet. Type in the word "protocol" and see how many seminars and schools are available to the business community, so they can be competitive in the global marketplace.

It is important to remember that becoming a person of honor doesn't happen at a seminar or by reading a book. It is a lifetime commitment. It is having a teachable spirit for the remainder of one's life. It is cultivating the skill of being humble enough to recognize that protocol and honor are necessary and doing what it takes to learn and practice protocol.

Warfare by Honor

Qaumaniq and I are not experts at protocol but we have committed ourselves to becoming persons of honor. We have made many mistakes in protocol ceremonies but we have been forgiven them because people know our hearts are for honor.

It may seem like there is a mountain of knowledge to climb but the largest obstacle is a true understanding of one's own arrogance and lack of humility. We all believe we are not arrogant and that we possess a generous amount of humility. The truth of these is always revealed when it comes time to honor others in a proper manner. Being a person of honor is mostly about consistency. While protocol is a ceremony, honor is character. It takes both to relate to others, especially those of differing cultures.

You might take a moment and ask yourself some questions about your level of cultural awareness. Create your own self-profile about cross-cultural relationships and your current knowledge of protocol. Think about committing to becoming a person of honor. Count the costs and advantages of investing in the education necessary to become a person of honor. Remember the times when your heart was full of honor for someone, but you lacked the skills to protocol them and reveal your heart to them.

Begin to get a vision of a family committed to honor and protocol. Begin to build an inventory of skills and practices, habits and actions that will become part of the spirit of your family, neighborhood, and community. Later in this book, Qaumaniq shares some wonderful stories of families who are pro-active in honor and protocol and what they do to promote it in their homes and lives.

Cross Cultural Awareness

Maybe you or your employer would like to have a protocol seminar in their place of business to improve their relational skills. Maybe a protocol seminar could be arranged for your community. Many resources are available for anyone willing to commit him or herself.. Remember this book is simply a key that unlocks a door but it doesn't open that door. Only you can open that door. Are you ready?

Warfare by Honor

Chapter Eleven

Some Protocol Ceremonies

1. A Welcoming Ceremony:

A. The venue host (ie. Church, conference, gathering, seminar, etc.) introduce the local indigenous leaders and gifts them. The indigenous leaders welcome everyone…..if there are special guests (speakers, leaders, etc.) the indigenous leaders welcome them;

1. To the land

2. To the tribe or people group

3. Release authority to the guests to do what they came to do

4. Offer them blessing and protection during their stay

5. Gift the guests with something from the tribe or people group (the gifts can include but are not limited to songs, crafts, regalia, jewelry, food, art, etc.)

B. The venue host introduces local, State, or national government leaders who then welcome the guests to the land (they may also bring gifts).

C. The venue host introduces the local or regional spiritual leaders who welcome the guests to the land (they may also bring gifts).

D. The guests receive the welcomes the gifts and return the protocol with their own gifts from their culture, tribe, or people. (in all cases, spouses are also gifted— always find out if there is a spouse involved!)

E. If at all possible, always gift in the order you were gifted (ie. indigenous people, local government, spiritual leaders, etc.). If possible, gift from the eldest to the youngest. It is permissible to inquire as to who the elders are in the venue.

2. Visiting a local authority (ie. chief, mayor, council chairman/woman, etc.)

A. Call or write to make an appointment (always be on time for any appointment!).

B. Collect information about the person(s) being visited; their titles, their spouse, their tribe or nation, what questions will be asked of you, what answers may be expected by those questions. If you intend to bring regalia as a gift, discreetly inquire as to size ("If I were to bring regalia, what sizes should I be prepared to bring?").

C. In all cases, when visiting a leader, let her/him be the first to speak.

D. In most cases, do not ask questions except for clarification ("What do you mean by your question to me about...?"). Let the leader ask the questions. She or he may ask you, "Do you have any questions?" Then it is appropriate to answer.

E. If you are visiting a tribe that is not your own or you are on some other tribal land, take time to explain that you are;

1. A visitor

2. That you possess no authority upon that land except what might be granted by the local authorities.

3. That you respect the local authorities and their gate-keepers (chiefs, chairman, council, etc.)

4. That you would seek their blessing to do what you came to do on their land, with their people.

5. That you would like to honor them with a protocol gift (If necessary, explain your gift—it would be dishonoring to them if they had to ask you, "why are you giving me this ostrich feather dipped in chocolate?")

6. Be patient and wait for the blessing. Give your host plenty of time to contemplate your request for blessing your visit on the land. Do not interrupt your host at any time, especially during the blessing time.

7. Thank your host for their blessing and assure your understanding if they, for whatever reason, cannot give it. Thank them for their consideration.

8. Keep your time brief and leave when the visit is over. Do not "hang" around their office or the meeting place.

9. If they should ask you to lunch or coffee time, make every effort to allow some extra time if they seek your accompaniment (if they ask you to lunch, they will most likely pay as you are now their guest— you may discreetly offer to pay your portion of the check but do not put up a fight over it—honor their desire to treat you with respect and honor—this meal may actually be their protocol gift to you).

F. If you are participating in a local venue (conference, seminar, meeting, etc.) be sure to invite your host, without pressure, informing her/him of the venue, time, place, and subject. Indicate your purpose to honor them with acknowledgement at the venue should they choose to attend. Assure them that it isn't necessary for them to attend the whole program if their schedule does not permit them to.

G. If the local leader(s) should come to your venue, make a place for introducing them, thanking them for their welcome, give them a chance to greet those attending, and present them with a gift, and thank them for coming to the venue. (Note: if they have indicated that they cannot stay for entire event, put their presentation at the beginning of the event and acknowledge to those attending that the leader(s) have a previous schedule they must maintain and graciously excuse them from the meeting (you might have those attending greet one another while you see the leader(s) to the door).

H. If the leader(s) attend your venue, do not embarrass them in any way. Do not draw undue attention to them by using them as examples, etc. Do not tell a joke on their tribe or make them to feel inferior in any way (because they are not!). At the close of your presentation you might gratefully acknowledge the presence of the leader(s).

I. Never forget to acknowledge a leaders spouse! If you brought only one gift, present it to them both. **Do not leave one of them out of the protocol!**

3. Attending a Potlatch

Giving makes us richer because through it we come to understand how our lives have been built on the generosity of our relations and ancestors.

Breining, Jeane (Haida) *Alaska Native Ways* (Portland, Oregon: Graphic Arts Center Publishing Co.,2002) p.123

A. Acknowledge that you received the invitation to attend the potlatch. If you are unable to attend, give a brief description of your reason and thank the host for the generous invitation to attend. Wish them well and send a protocol gift to the host.

B. If you attend a potlatch, arrive on schedule, ask if there is parking for the visitors but do not park where the hosts or elders would be parking.

C. Ask if there are protocol instructions for the potlatch and/or a schedule of events.

D. During the feasts never decline what is offered on your plate. Be sure to try a little of everything. Do not throw anything away as many times the elders will retrieve what is not consumed. A potlatch is a time of extravagant feasting and you may feel like you're about to burst but the proper protocol is to be at the feasts, on time, in your place, and ready to eat (we might suggest you take a walk to settle your meals rather than take a nap).

E. When you enter the feast hall (a gym, long-house, tribal building, etc.) do not take a seat up front but take a humble seat. The elders generally sit near the front. One of the hosts may come and offer you a seat of honor near the front, graciously accept their offer.

F. The hosting family or tribe will be serving the feast. Be sure to thank every server as they present their food to you.

G. Speeches by the chiefs, hosts, and elders usually follows the feasting time. Do not leave until it is clear the feast time is over. Sometimes a dance will follow and that is a good way to settle your meal.

H. Remember a potlatch is an investment (sometimes for their future) manifested by a great food outlay, a generous amount of gift giving, and time spent gathering the food and making the gifts.

Some Protocol Ceremonies

I. Usually the last evening is the time of gift giving. Everyone invited to the potlatch receives a gift. Sometimes a host will honor someone specifically with a special gift for her/him. Receive what you are presented and be thankful to your host. (A note of explanation about the potlatch; many native villages did not have any stores for shopping or even trading posts in the old days so the potlatch served as a means, not only of honoring, but of the disbursement and sharing of goods. One of the native values can be said like this: It's not the amount one can hoard but the amount one is willing to give away that makes one wealthy. This value was unacceptable to the immigrants and there was a time when the potlatch was outlawed and natives were imprisoned for dancing and gift giving. The potlatch is being practiced today in both Alaska and Canada.)

J. Leave a potlatch in a humble way, with a grateful heart that you were a part of a life experience most others will never experience in their lifetimes. A potlatch gives one time to examine their own generosity and the reasons they are gathering material goods. It is also an example of a time in the future when the Great Creator will host a universal potlatch. He sent an invitation to attend that special potlatch with His son. It does, however, require an r.s.v.p.

K. A thank you card should be sent to the person(s) who secured your invitation to the potlatch.

There are many ceremonies and cultural celebrations happening all during the year. Attend some of them and make it a family event. Learn about other people and their cultures. Create some of your own ceremonies for your family, tribe, and nation. Every ceremony began with some creative idea from some creative person. Qaumaniq writes some really great examples in the chapter, *Establishing Protocol in the Home.*

Remember, ceremonial protocol could begin with you.

Chapter Twelve

Establishing Protocol
in the Home

I swear I will not dishonor my soul with hatred, but offer myself
humbly as a guardian of nature, as a healer of misery, as
a messenger of wonder, and as an architect of peace.
School Prayer by Diane Ackerman

When we teach on Protocol we are often asked the question, "Where do I begin to restore honor/protocol in my home and my life?" Interestingly enough, most people are implementing protocol already and are unaware of it.

We have compiled some examples of our own lives and people that we know to show you how easy it is to begin the process of reestablishing honor in our everyday lives. These examples can be utilized by you, but it is also very rewarding to ask the Creator to give to you your own creative ideas concerning ways in which to honor others. Being the very essence of honor, He has an infinite array of ideas, that when put into action, can bring life and restoration to others through the simple act of honor. May these following stories inspire you to become people of protocol.

Steve and Susan Nichols

Steve and Susan were childless for many years. Their greatest desire was to have a large family in which to share the love that the Creator, Yahweh, had gifted to them when He brought them together. After many years, they began the process of adoption and Yahweh has increased their home with 3 sons and a daughter. Steve and Susan are already instilling within their children the concept of honor as a way of life. At night, when they tuck their children into bed, they guide their children in a prayer for their future mate. They pray for that mate, still a child, wherever they may be, that Yahweh will watch over them until He brings them together when they are older. This, in and of itself, is an honorable act, but they do not stop there.

At the end of the year, they take their sons to purchase sterling silver charms. Their sons pick out 3 that represent special aspects of that year for them. One year, the oldest two sons bought footballs since this was the year that they began to play football. One bought a dog, since that year they got their dog. And then they come home with their 3 charms and write a letter telling what they did that year, and talk about their lives.

Steve and Susan keep these charms and the letters in a safe place and add to them every year. They are preparing for the day when their sons are gifted one of the greatest gifts that the

Creator can bestow upon them, the gift of their wife. Steve and Susan will then buy a sterling silver charm bracelet. On the day of the wedding, they will present this bracelet to the bride of their son. After the wedding, their son will present to His new bride all the charms of his life, along with the letters he has written over the years, many in the handwriting of a child. In this act of honor and love, he will be presenting himself to her, along with his history, and she will see how he has prepared himself for her, over many years. Steve and Susan will have given her the bracelet that holds all these precious memories, and in doing so, will be welcoming this new person into their family and protocoling her with the greatest gift of all, their son. They will have honored her by guiding their son, over the years, toward this day. They will have taught each son to pray for their wife, to save themselves for her, and to give of themselves to her, the totally of themselves, including their history. What a welcome! What an act of Protocol!

Doyle and Dani Baggett

Doyle and Dani have two daughters, Sarah and Hannah. One day when I, Qaumaniq, was riding in the car with Dani and her girls, she began to follow the car in front of us and when I asked her what she was doing she said, "You'll see, just trust me."

She followed this elderly man into his subdivision and when he went inside his house, she pulled in the driveway, parked, went to the front door and knocked on the door. The man's wife answered the door and she said, "Maam, I noticed that your husband is a veteran by the tag on his car. Could we step in and have a word with him?" The woman said that would be fine and we stepped inside the room, where the man was sitting. Dani introduced herself to the man and then she said these words, "Sir, I noticed that you are a veteran and I wanted to stop in and thank you for the sacrifice that you have made for us so that my daughters and I could live in safety and freedom. I want my daughters to know that you and other veterans are worthy of great honor and respect." The man wept. No one had ever thanked him.

Judith Woodall:

I have known Judith for many years. From the day that her two children were born, she has been writing a journal about their lives. Each journal has the history of their lives, completely full of memories, her prayers, and promises that the Creator has spoken to her concerning her children. What a gift to give, not only to them, but the generations to come. She has compiled a history of their lives so that future generations can utilize it to learn about their ancestry.

Rosemary Stanley

Some years ago, my mother was awarded teacher of the year for her school district. As a child, when I would meet people and they would find out that my mother was Rosemary Stanley, the teacher, they would rave about her. I am convinced that my mother was successful, not only for her ability, but because she was a woman who sowed honor in all her relationships.

My mother has now retired after 53 years of teaching kindergarten. She still goes to read to the children daily. Every year, during the time of high school graduation, she plans a party for the graduating seniors that she had as students in kindergarten. She sends out invitations to invite them to an "evening with Mrs. Stanley." At the gathering, she allows each one to tell of their future plans, and she tells them wonderful memories that she has of them as five-year-old children. She displays pictures of them from days gone by, when they were in her class. She also presents them with some of their art work that she has saved for them over the twelve years. What a special blessing for these children to see the value that they have been to my mother. They are reminded that they are not forgotten but are cherished.

Another story, that reveals the honorable character of my mother, touches my heart every time I repeat the story. Some years back my mother had a young boy in her kindergarten class. He came to school carrying a little guitar, wearing his cowboy boots, and cowboy hat. He told my mom that he wanted to be a country music star. My mother could have scoffed or even laughed it off as a childish dream. Instead, she marched that little boy down to the office of the school and said to the school secretary and principle, "This is Ken. He is a country music star, so I think that we need to let him sing over the microphone on the school P.A. system this morning." Ken sang his heart out and many years later that same young man became a country music entertainer. When Country Music Television did a documentary about Ken, he asked that they interview my mother. He said that, next to his parents, my mother had made the greatest impact on his life. The television interviewer asked my mother why she did that for Ken and she replied, "I knew that he was an entertainer. I saw that the day he brought in his guitar. God places the gifts within children, all we have to do is simply call forth those gifts." My mother's classroom was a place of honor and children received the same honor as adults were given. They were not devalued because they were little people. To my mother, all people are worthy of honor.

My mother also passed down a protocol of honor that I still retain today. When one of her friends would have a baby, we would always go to see the new baby with a gift. Many people will visit a new baby. The difference in my mother's visit is that she would not take a gift for the new baby, instead she would take gifts for the older children. I remember when I asked her "Why do you do that?" she said, "The new baby is too little to know that they are being honored and they will not remember the visit. However, the older children are old enough to remember and to recognize the honor. They have stood by while people have gushed over this little baby and they probably feel left out and a bit rejected. I want to gift them so that they will not feel replaced. I think that will help them not to feel jealous of their new sibling." I remember thinking this was so great of my mom.

When I was growing up, my mother always honored our birthdays. This was a day of celebration at our house. She wanted us to know that we were wanted and loved. On our birthdays, we got to choose our favorite dinner and she would prepare it for us. When we would come to the table for our celebration, there would be a big poster that said our name and the words "This is your life!" On the poster would be pictures of us from birth all through the years of our lives. This was such an honor for me and for my brother's.

On the day that I won cheerleader at my school, I called my mom to tell her about it. That was two hours before I was to return home for the day. I was shocked when I came into the house to see balloons and a cake that said "Congratulations

Cheerleader!" My mom made it a point to honor us on a regular basis.

Suuqiina

When Suuqiina was a pastor, he instructed his congregation on giving to the poor or less fortunate. He told them not to give their hand-me-down clothes, that were worn out, or to give food they would not eat. Instead, he suggested that when they were buying clothes for themselves or their family, to buy an extra item of clothing that was new and give that to the poor. He also told them to buy extra food during their regular shopping but to make sure that they choose food that they would want to eat and give that to the poor. He challenged his congregation to honor the poor by investing in them financially and by treating them as they would like to be treated themselves. This may sound like common sense to the readers of this book, however, many times the poor are dishonored in the process of giving to them. In the past, used teabags have been sent to the Indian reservations, and also two left shoes. We need to be honorable in our giving.

Suuqiina has honored me repeatedly, by standing up for me when I am devalued as a woman in ministry. When he proposed to me he said, "I am going to be a platform that you can dance on." Because of the male-valued religious system in which we work, he continues to face the devaluing of women on a regular basis. When we are in ministry meetings and he is introduced as the speaker and I am left out, he corrects this by saying, "Qaumaniq and I are a team and we present together." When he is given protocol gifts and I am left out he says, "I receive this for Qaumaniq and myself because we are one." He makes sure that people know of my contribution to our ministry and my active place along side him. This has cost him a comfortable seat in the 'good ole boys club' as he has been left out of the circle, at times, because of the stand he takes to honor me, and in standing for the honoring of women in general.

When Suuqiina asked me to marry him, he lived in Alaska and I lived in Tennessee. After he asked me, he returned home to Alaska. He asked me not to answer until I heard from the Lord and until I received something that he would be sending to me. Upon his return to Alaska, he stayed up one whole night and composed a betrothal book for me. In the book were poems that he had written, along with pictures of his photography and oil paintings. There were also pictures of him, when he was a young boy, in the orphanage. Along the way in the book, he would write hand written messages of love to me. The book is a beautiful compilation of his soul on paper. It was an incredible honor to receive it and I will always cherish the book, and the honorable way that he asked me to share in his life.

As a pastor, Suuqiina instructed his Sunday school teachers to alert parents of children that showed an interest in receiving Yeshua. He asked the teachers to refrain from leading the children to salvation themselves, but to allow the parents the honor and privilege to lead their own children to Him. That's the way of honor.

Debbie Davenport

Debbie is a single mom who has worked, diligently, to keep her family intact after experiencing a divorce that she did not want. She believes that traditions are an important part of keeping a family together and that such traditions give the family meaning and purpose. On Christmas day, she and her children have a tradition of making sugar cookies together and preparing a breakfast meal. I have known her to stay up all night preparing food, wrapping gifts, and adding special last minute touches for her children. In all the years that I have known her, I have never known her to miss the sugar cookie tradition.

It is not about sugar cookies, it is about the process of gathering together as a family to make life long memories. When I am able, I stop over at the Davenport's on Christmas and it brings joy to my heart when I see the plate of traditional sugar cookies on the table. Once again, Debbie has won the battle that she has been fighting for the last several years. That battle being the ability to leave her children with memories that they can cherish and traditions to hang on to in a world system that has little value for lasting traditions, ones that build security and belonging to it's children. Debbie is one of my heroes for her tenacity in holding on to what was important to her, before the divorce, and refusing to let go of her values.

The Jewish people have done this for generations, by holding on to Shabbat and the Feasts of the Lord. I have been told that they kept the Shabbat (Sabbath) while they were in the concentration camps, during the holocaust. These traditions, given to them by Yahweh, kept them as a people. It is an honorable and necessary act to pass our traditions on to our children and grandchildren.

Susan Allen-Hudgins

When I was a teenager, I used to visit a friend of mine named Susan. Her home was always a hang out for teens. We loved to be there. As I look back on that time, with what I now know about honor, I understand why we loved to be there. Susan's family had a large table that seated many people. On that table there was a white table cloth. The first time you would eat at that table as a guest, you would be asked to sign your name on the table cloth. Later, Susan's mother would embroidery the names on the table cloth in different colors. The table cloth was filled with colorful names of all the people that had been served at the table. I will never forget how honored I felt to sign my name on that cloth, alongside other important people of the city. In this simple act, the Allen's honored their guests by adding their names, permanently, at their table.

Dwight and Kimberly Jarratt

Dwight and Kimberly have a special plate they pull out for guests when they join them at their table for a meal. Their children love to pull out the plate for their guests.

Another way the Jarratts sow honor in their community is through acts of service and giving. When Dwight and Kimberly purchased their new automobile, instead of trading in their used car, they gave it to a Kurdish family that did not have an automobile.

At one time, Kimberly kept boxes of clothes in her storage building that she would pass on to people who needed clothes. She also bakes some killer chocolate chip cookies and she is known for delivering these cookies to hospitals, homes of sick, or bereaved people. I have known her to tuck her five children into bed and head out on a night-time run to the hospital to check on some one or deliver a baked care package.

When I lived with the Jarratts, I was constantly amazed at their commitment to help others who were less fortunate than them. I watched them do this in an honoring way, that left the receiver of their benevolence feeling loved and supported, never less-than or as a "mission project." Many times I was the recipient of their support and good will. When I would come to Kimberly with a problem or challenge she would say, "We will make it work." I have always said that Kimberly could take dirt and make it into a work of art.

The Jarratt family ministered to me when I was very ill for several years. Before I moved in with them, Kimberly would bring her children to my home to vacuum and do odd chores. Sometimes she would take me to my doctor appointments or pick up food for me at the store. I will never forget how, after her visits to my home, I would find encouraging scripture cards the children had decorated, taped to my cabinets and mirrors.

The Jarratts have included their children in the process of honoring others and, in so doing, have passed this gift of honor on to their children, who are as committed to serving others as they have been.

Dwight and Kimberly often plan surprise get away trips for each other. With a large family, they have learned the importance of continuing to work on their marriage and relationship. On Dwight's 30th birthday, Kimberly called all of their friends and asked them to dress up like old people and come to a surprise party for him. Another time, she surprised him with a trip to Atlanta for a ball game. She arranged, with his boss for him travel to Atlanta, to what he thought was a work-related meeting. She went to the airport in disguise, loaded with makeup and a wig. Once they were seated on the plane, she struck up a conversation with him and when he saw that it was Kimberly in this ridiculous get up, he died laughing. Kimberly went to a lot of work to pull this off and it affirmed

Dwight of his value in Kimberly's heart. This trip created a fun memory and it honored him. One can see the love involved to put the time and thought into this act.

What is even more impressive, is the fact that it had only been a couple years since Dwight and Kimberly had lost their two year old daughter in a drowning accident. Dwight and Kimberly's commitment to continue to show up for one another, actively pursue ways to honor and celebrate one another and their marriage, is not only honorable, it is courageous.

I like to think of new ways to honor the people I love and also those who I may not know well. It is exciting and rewarding to see the faces of those who are honored respond with smiles, tears of joys, and looks of dignity as shame is removed from them. We can all be ambassadors of hope and can combat this spirit of terrorism that has swept our world. What follows are some things in which I have been privileged to participate. At the time, these things may seem small and inconsequential, in the big scheme of things. However, if we all do our small part, to sow honor in our part of the world, we will see great things happen and will reap a mighty harvest in the generations to come. It is now more crucial than ever that we are committed to this task.

Our Public Servants

On 9-11 we suddenly became aware of the firefighters, police, and emergency personnel who put their lives on the line everyday, to protect us in our country. Up until that time, unless you had a loved one in that line of work, you were probably unaware of the benefits that these courageous, often invisible people, awarded to us. Since that time, Suuqiina and

Establishing Protocol in the Home

I make every effort to affirm those people, whenever we see them in public. It might be a soldier, a fireman, or a police officer. Whenever we come upon one in our daily schedule, we stop and thank them for the sacrifice they make so that we might live in peace and safety. We thank them and tell them we sleep better at night knowing that they are there. We are amazed how often many of them tell us that we are the first people to ever have thanked them. How sad it is that these people, who are put in harms way so our quality of life might be vastly improved, are overlooked.

Some of our First Nations people have started a ministry to honor the veterans of the United States. It is called the 'Warriors Medal of Valor.' This ministry has designed some beautiful medallions that we purchase from them. They come with a certificate to present to veterans who are special to us. We take these medallions and make a beaded necklace (native style) on which to hang them. They are simply elegant. The certificate that we frame for them reads:

Warriors Medal of Valor

From The Native American Nations of the United States of America let it be known to all persons who view this certifi -cate that the following person is hereby awarded the Warriors Medal of Valor for valorous service while serving in the United States of America in a military capacity. This conspicuous performance of duty represents great patriot -ism and pride in the finest traditions of the Untied States Armed Forces and reflects great credit upon the recipient and their military service. It is with great respect that the Native American Nations of the United States of America hereby present the Warriors Medal of Valor. We are grateful for your service.

A Viet Nam veteran told us this was one of the few acts of honor that he has received. The lack of honor that our veterans receive, when they return home after serving our country and laying down their lives, can be so disheartening. It can make reentry into our nation increasingly difficult, causing a sense of abandonment, isolation, and depression. Our veterans are due honor and we are grossly negligent if we refuse, through our own ignorance and self-absorption, to release to them what is rightfully theirs.

"Our veterans are due honor and we are grossly negligent if we refuse...to release to them what is rightfully theirs."

Honoring of Children

One of the things that Suuqiina and I are challenged with is how to be involved, on a regular basis, in the lives of our grandchildren, since they are all spread out across the U.S. and not near where we live. One of the things that we do, on a regular basis, is to send them gifts by mail. There is a discount store, in almost every city where we travel, called *The Dollar Tree*, and we frequent it on a regular basis. Because everything in the store is a dollar, we can get a cart load of little surprises for our grandchildren at a reasonable price. Children love to get mail. We send these little gifts to them from time to time as "Just Because" gifts. "Just Because" we love you. For the young children, we include a picture of ourselves so they can make the connection between the gifts and who sent them.

When we meet children in our ministry meetings, we encourage them to send us their art-work and letters and become pen pals. When we are in local churches and we give protocol gifts to the pastoral couples, we try to include their children in the gifting process. When the children write to us and send us artwork, we try to respond to each of them with a short note. We want them to feel they are important in the Kingdom of Yahweh because they are.

Honoring and Supporting Widows and Orphans (Single Moms and Their Children)

One of the ways that I have honored single moms in the past is to help out during the holidays, with financial support. All parents want to gift their children and it can be more than disheartening when you have little or nothing to give them.

Several years ago, I had a friend, with three children, who was in the midst of a divorce she did not want. She was over-whelmed, to the point that she could not bear to face the shopping malls, and didn't have the energy to pull off Christmas for her children by herself. I had her make a list of what gifts she would like to get her children and a wish list for herself. I got on the phone and summoned the help of the Body of Christ. We pooled our money together and had more than enough to provide everything on her list. I did the shopping and she wrapped the gifts. On Christmas Eve, I placed her wish list gifts under the tree, including a special pearl ring with a letter that affirmed and encouraged her to trust in Yahweh, as she walked through this challenging and sorrowful time.

At the next Christmas she was stronger and ready to tackle the holiday shopping, so I gathered offerings and turned the money over to her to do her own shopping. That year I had her make out a wish list for herself and I went to the store and purchased everything on her list. I made some fake money and told her to have her children do chores around the house and to pay them with the fake money. This way the children could earn the gifts that they would purchase for her. After a few weeks of earning fake money for chores they did, I set up a "store" in one upstairs bedroom and put out all the things that I had purchased from her list. The children came over and spent their fake money on gifts for their mom. They were so proud of the gifts they had earned for her. The adjoining bedroom was filled with wrapping paper and bows and they wrapped their own gifts for their mom.

I spent the first few years, on Christmas morning, with this family. I would go over for a traditional breakfast and stay with the mom until the children left to be with their dad. It can be a very sad time for divorced parents on holidays, when they have to be without their children, and a good friend can be a great support to help combat the loneliness.

One year, a few months into the divorce, I could see that my friend was having an emotional meltdown. Overwhelmed with the new responsibilities of running a household alone, along with the profound grief of the loss of a partner, she needed support. I contacted several local Christian believers and we decided to bombard her with blessings for a solid week. Some people sent flowers, one sent a coupon for a pedicure, one changed the oil in her car, one mowed her lawn, many brought her meals for a week, some brought groceries, one gave her a bird feeder, some sent cards with money. The believers in this community poured out love upon this woman and, her children were greatly encouraged as well. What a great witness it was for the children to see the church work as a vessel of hope.

A few years after the divorce, I listened as my friend shared her sadness about her exhusband affording great vacations for the children but her salary, as a woman reentering the work place, did not afford her the ability to provide this memory for her children. I got on the phone, and once again the Body of believers in our area pooled together the money, to send her and her children to Florida for a week, the price of a rental car, and spending money. Years later, she tells me that this is one of the best memories that she and her children have together. I am so glad that we put our resources together to invest in this priceless gift.

Another time I watched as my friend struggled, as a single mom, to make repairs on her home. Many times, she was running to the library to get 'how to' books to learn how to make needed repairs that she could not afford. She wanted her home to be a source of pride and not shame for her children. One year, I decided to call together a group of people to have a "work day" at her house. Several us came together and we painted, did plumbing, and made necessary repairs. I will never forget how excited the children were to have us in the home helping out. It greatly encouraged them.

It is not difficult to find ways to help single parents, mothers and fathers. Most of the time they are overwhelmed and all you have to do is observe and you will find a need to meet. It is important that as you do minister to these families, you do not leave them feeling as is they are the "mission field" or that you are earning your "angel's wings" for your benevolence. I have found that in honoring them, I was the one profoundly blessed and they, in turn, sowed greatly into my life.

Celebrating Life through Blessing Parties

Blessing parties are a special way to celebrate the gift of life that a friend or family brings to you. I have given blessing parties and have had a blessing party given in my honor. They are powerful.

One such party that I remember was for my friend Tami. Tami is by nature a soft spoken, kind, and loyal friend. She was also the leader and founder of a worship dance ministry in our church. One year, I planned a surprise birthday party for her. I enlisted the help of her mother and husband to pull off the surprise. I wrote, inviting people to come and bring a gift, but to also bring a written letter of blessing for Tami. The letter would contain special memories they have of Tami, descriptions of the gifts that Tami brings to the Body of Christ, and scriptures that would encourage her. They would also express what they would like to see for Tami in her future. I purchased a cake for her and everyone brought refreshments. When Tami arrived, she was quite surprised. The special surprise that we had for her, however, was something from our hearts. As the director of the dance ministry, Tami had received many dances that were inspired by Yahweh. She taught them to

"Blessing parties are a special way to celebrate the gift of life that a friend or family brings to you."

us who were on her dance team. Over the years, we had shared these worship dances in our church to glorify the Lord Yeshua.

At Tami's blessing party, as a part of the worship, the dance team did each of the dances that Tami had taught us, so that she could participate as an observer (something she had never been able to do since she was always leading us in the dances). Tami got to see what a blessing these dances were to the Lord and to the Body of Christ, and we honored her for the contribution that she made through her gifting of worship dance.

We can honor our friends and family for the gifts that they bring to our lives and to Yahweh. It is not exalting men, it is a simple act of honor and it is biblical.

Honoring Leaders and Their Spouses

Several years ago I wanted to do something special for the spiritual leaders in our city. It seemed they were always giving to others but that they were due something special, to thank them for their contributions to the community.

I decided to host a Pastoral Couple's dinner in my home, bringing together pastoral couples in the city. I wanted to honor them and to give them the opportunity to get to know one another, in a neutral place, where they could move across denominational lines and differences.

I moved all of the furniture out of my living room and set up card tables with tablecloths and floral arrangements. I added candles to the tables, to give it the feel of fine dining. I enlisted the help of friends and we put together a "five star" meal to serve to the couples. One of my friends picked up the children to take to her home, providing childcare for the night, free of charge.

As the couples came in and were seated, the wives were given long stemmed roses.

That night, my friends and I served these couples as if they were in a fine and expensive restaurant. We pulled out all the stops so they would feel nurtured, special, and honored. After the meal, we removed the tables and seated them in a large circle. My friends and I shared our hearts of gratitude for the contributions and sacrifices that each couple had made to our community. Then we encouraged them to share with one another, pastor to pastor, their hopes, dreams, disappointments, and prayer requests. The meeting was a simple act of honor but went far beyond our expectations in touching these leaders hearts, and beginning the process of unifying our city as the true Body of Christ.

A few years back, an international couple in leadership came to our city and I agreed to book ministry meetings for them, take care of their housing, and transportation while they were in the area.

We had two weeks of life changing meetings, and it was a time of bonding between us. While they were with me, I took a small tape recorder along and recorded their messages and special words that they had concerning our city. I made little verbal notes on the recorder to remind myself of special things, so I would not forget. I also took along a camera and lots of film. After they returned to their home, I spent several days creating a special scrapbook for them of memories that we made together, while they were in my city. The recorder helped me to specifically document their visit and the pictures brought the words to life. I mailed it to them to have as a special memento to keep, so they could remember how important they were to many people in our city.

Honoring the Memory of Others

One of the greatest honors we can give a deceased person is to remember them. When our granddaughter died, I learned this. As each day went by we felt further and further from her. At times we wished to suspend time, so we didn't have to face the future. It seemed we were leaving her memory behind. We also came to understand the overwhelming need to have her life mean something. In other words, we did not want her to be forgotten. The greatest blessing, to our family, is when people remember her in some small and yet meaningful way.

"The greatest blessing, to our family, is when people remember her in some small and yet meaningful way."

When we speak our message on Israel and how Yahweh longs for His first-born child, we share the story of Allie and how we bare a portion of the pain He feels when longing for His child, Israel. It brings us comfort to share the message about Allie's death, when we speak about Israel. It helps to keep her memory alive to us.

Next year we will begin a project in Allie's honor. We are building a gathering place on our property that will house worship, art shows, and where we will gather to celebrate the feasts of the Lord. We are going to build paths in the woods, along side the gathering place, that have meditation benches.

We will dedicate this building in honor of Allie and it is our prayer that many people will come to our land, find peace and shalom in the building we dedicate in her honor. We want this healing place to reflect what Allie's life represents to us as her family.

We have done the same thing for two other families in our lives. The Baggatts lost their daughter to leukemia after a six-year battle. We hung her picture in our motor home and dedicated the motor home in her honor. As we travel the highways and byways, bringing the good news, we take Hannah Baggett along with us. Her smiling face reminds us, everyday, to not take life for granted. Hannah wanted to be a missionary to children. She was not able to fulfill her wish to the fullness in which she longed. When we wrote our children's book, we dedicated the book to Hannah and her family. It is a connection to the children of the world that we wanted to fulfill for her. Even in eternity, she still impacts her world. This simple act brought great comfort to her family.

We also had a First Nations friend named Deborah Conklin who was killed in a car accident with her sixteen-year-old daughter, Meagan. We received a 16" by 20" photo of Deborah and Meagan from her husband. We have plans to build an art gallery on our land and will hang this picture in the gallery. We will dedicate the gallery in the honor of Deborah and Meagan. Along side the picture of them, we have a framed piece of words that Deborah shared about her heart for the First Nation's people.

A simple act of honor toward a family that has lost a loved one, is to mark your calendar with the birthday of the deceased and the anniversary of their death. A card or flowers can mean so much.

Establishing Protocol in the Home

This year I got Allie's mother, Hannah's mother, and a friend together to join me, around the time of Allie's and Hannah's birthdays. It just so happened to be on Hannah's special day. We ordered a cake, spoke our memories of the girls, and sang happy birthday to them, to honor them. Allie's mom and Hannah's mom both cried as they spoke of their loss, how they missed their girls, but both gained strength by being able to celebrate their lives and share their birthdays with special friends.

Miscarriages and still-born births can be so difficult, due to the fact that most people do not know how to deal with this since there is usually not a funeral. We can help families by remembering them during these times. We can deliver food, help with child-care, lend a listening ear, and allow them to grieve. Once, when one of my friends had a miscarriage, I called on her and carried her a long stem red rose. I danced a dance of mourning for her and her child, and at the end of the dance, I handed her the rose. For one of my friends that had a stillborn child, I planned and led a ceremony for the family. They were allowed to share their grief and feelings about their child. We read scriptures of comfort and had a time of worship together. It was a time to come together to show them our support.

Honoring Traditions for the Family

When my children were growing up, I wanted to instill in them a sense of honoring and caring for others. In our city, every year, there is a program called "Christmas For Kids." The bus drivers for the country music stars have a week where they display the motor coaches, to the public, for a fee. Then at Christmas, K-mart closes it doors at 6 p.m., to allow under privileged children a special treat. The bus drivers pick these children up at school and transport them to a dinner feast. After this, they load them back on the buses and head to K-mart. Our family, and other families from the city gather at the front of the store and watch as rows and rows of buses, decorated with Christmas lights, enter the parking lot. The buses come in blowing their horns and flashing their lights, with kids faces pressed to the windows.

After the buses park, the children unload and families are assigned a child to escort through the store. Each child is given a $75 credit at the checkout with which to purchase Christmas gifts.

Several years in a row our family participated in this program. It was the highlight of our holiday. It brought us back to the meaning of the holiday, the gift of giving. It developed character in my children that will last a life time.

One year we sponsored a person at the local nursing home and took her gifts on Christmas morning.

When our son was graduating from high school, we video-taped messages of blessing from fathers and mothers of the graduating class, for each graduate. We took photos of their lives, from the time they were babies until the present, played inspirational music in the background. The taped "blessing" messages from the parents, to every graduate, were played across a screen. The parents and the graduates were so blessed to have this played for all to see, and the video was made available for every family.

When our son became engaged, we had a special private meeting with him and his fiancé, and we gifted her with a special ring and gift. We welcomed her into our family and told her that we saw her as a special gift that Yahweh was giving to us. We let her know that she is needed and wanted in our family. There would be far less trouble with in-laws if we would simply include the significant others of our children. Rejection and feeling "left out" is a powerful thing, and can cause hurt feelings that can last for a lifetime. An ounce of prevention is worth a pound of cure. In our family, we go out of our way to help the newer members of the family to feel as equally important as the historical ones. We try not to talk about a history they are not part of. We want them to feel intrinsically vital in our family unit.

> *"Establishing honor can be as simple as giving credit to others for the contributions that they make in our lives."*

It is important to lead our children in developing these traditions in our families that honor others. We lead the way by example.

Establishing honor can be as simple as giving credit to others for the contributions that they make in our lives. When Suuqiina and I are sharing in ministry meetings, if we share a revelation that has been given to us by someone else, we always try to remember to give credit to those individuals and not lead people to believe that they are our own personal revelations.

When we moved into the area of our city, we visited the local mayor's office and took him a gift. We told him that we wanted to be a blessing in our city, and that we honored his authority and the contribution that he was making in our lives and of those in our city. He was surprised that we would take the time to do this. No one had ever done this before. What a blessing it would be if believers would take the time to visit local authorities and simply thank them for their work.

As Suuqiina and I travel and go about our daily business, if we come across an employee that serves us well, we stop and thank them. We also ask to speak to the manager and affirm the employee to the manager. Many times I will write a letter to the corporate offices of the employee, to affirm them and tell the office of the good service we received. I encourage the corporation to reward the person for their good service and I always send a copy of my letter to the employee, so they can see that they have been honored. In the service industry, today, people get far more complaints that affirmations. As spiritual people, it is important to be agents of encouragement to those along our path. Our words and gestures of honor may make the difference in their lives between life or death, success or failure, hope or despair.

I remember hearing a story that in a counseling meeting that I will never forget. There was a lady, in my counseling group, who was wealthy and well respected in the community. I could have never dreamed the environment that she came from in light of where she is in her life today.

She shared with us that, as a child, she grew up in the inner city of a large community in the Southeast. She lived in the poor housing area for those on welfare. Her mother was a prostitute, her sister was a prostitute, one brother was in jail for murder, and another brother was in jail for rape.

When she was about eight years old, she was invited to participate in a city-wide project for poor children. The children were taught how to do a woodworking project. After the project was completed, the local newspaper came to do a story about the children. The photographer from the newspaper took a picture of the children with their crafts. The lady told us that this photographer walked over to her and said, "Look around you. See all the death in this place? You are different from this. You do not belong here. You are going to make something good of your life. I can tell you are special with a special plan for your life." This woman said the words of this man stuck with her the entirety of her childhood, and the words of this man set her destiny. She not only walked a different path from the destruction of the rest of her family, she became a successful, spiritual woman. This photographer took a moment of his time and affirmed a small child with words of honor, and it changed her destiny. Small acts of kindness that are sown can reap a powerful outcome in the lives of others.

Each one of us has the power to create, given to us by our Creator. Take the time to establish a plan to restore honor in your home and life. It is incredibly rewarding and it releases blessings to your family that are transferable throughout the generations. What could be more rewarding, at the end of your life, than to have people say, "You are a person of honor!"

Warfare by Honor

Chapter Thirteen

The Protocol of Elohim Concerning Israel

For God's gifts and His call are irrevocable.

Romans 11:17-29

Several years ago I was very ill. I had been bed ridden off and on for most of a year. During that time, as I began to improve a bit, Jesus spoke to my heart and asked me a question.. He said, "Will you go to Israel?" My answer was swift. "Why on earth would I want to travel to a war torn country while suffering with a horrible disease? I was still very weak, was taking multiple medications, I had no funds, and I was afraid to travel.

I told this to the Lord in prayer and yet His question persisted, "Will you go to Israel?" I could not for the life of me figure out why He was so persistent about Israel. After all the terrible things they had done. They had broken all His commandments, as if I had not done so as well. They were so disobedient that they were thrown out of their own land, and they had rejected my savior. Surely, they as a people group, had committed the unpardonable sin, and in my mind, the best that could happen to them was to make it through the tribulation, after I was "raptured" out of here. Or so I thought.

My thought process was not just the result of an arrogant and prideful heart. I had been taught this reasoning in the churches I had attended over the years. Sometimes it was blatant and sometimes it was subtle, but it was always the same message. The message was "the Christian church had replaced the Jews, and all the promises that were given to the Jews now belonged, exclusively, to the church."

So in light of this, you can understand why I was surprised at the persistence of Jesus concerning these very people, who, in my mind, had rejected Him.

Then He spoke the words that I will never forget. He spoke with kindness and clarity, as He by-passed my brain and went straight to my heart. He said, "You don't have to go to Israel. I will still love you and you will still be my girl. It's just that we are getting married and I would like you to meet my people."

I replied in astonishment, "You are a Jew!" In that one instant, He went from a White, Anglo-Saxon, Protestant, Republican, to a tribal man, a man of color, the Lion of the Tribe of Judah. My beloved was and is a Jew. I will never forget that moment in my life. It is one of the most profound experiences that I have ever experienced, and with that revelation of my Jewish savior, I entered into the prophetic destiny for my life.

The Protocol of Elohim Concerning Israel

Once I saw, with the eyes of my heart, that I was marrying a Jewish man, I could not wait to get to Israel. The fears that I had about the trip and the limitations that had been so large in my mind soon began to fade. I was a woman betrothed, in love with her husband to be, and I could not wait to set my feet on His land, and to gaze into the eyes of His people. I wanted to experience the place where He grew up as a child, the culture that He knew, and I wanted to taste the food He ate and smell the air that He breathed. I was smitten.

When my plane pulled into the airport in Tel Aviv, Israel, I placed a wedding veil on my head. As weird as it may sound, it was an intimate and symbolic act for me. As soon as I placed it on my head, the Jewish people around me said, "Are you getting married in Israel?" I said with excitement, "Yes, I am! My father has arranged the marriage and I am so excited. I can't wait to meet my groom. I have been reading His love letters for many years and now I am going to see His face and meet His people!"

I got off the plane in Israel wearing a wedding veil and I came home wearing an Israeli army uniform, with the rank provided to me by a Commander in the Israeli army. I was the warrior bride of Jesus, who I found out was called Yehshua by His people.

This experience broke replacement theology, the belief that the church has replaced Israel in the heart and promises of Yahweh, right off my mind and heart. I never really knew what replacement theology was or that it had its clutches around my heart until it was gone. Once it was gone, I could really see and experience the scriptures and my savior in a way I had never been able to experience before. You might say I had been "delivered."

While on my trip to Israel, I met with Arni and Yonit Klein for the first time. They were in the process of establishing a continuous worship center in Tel Aviv. They were radical worshippers and some of the most passionate people for Yeshua I had ever met.

While on the trip, Arni and Yonit ministered to our team. Arni was sharing with our group about Yahweh's heart for Israel, and He opened a scripture to us of which I was not aware. The scripture was Genesis 12:2-3 and it reads, "I will make you into a great nation and I will bless you; I will make your name great, and you will be a blessing. I will bless those who bless you, and whoever curses you I will curse; and all the peoples on the earth will be blessed through you."

Arni told us that the literal Hebrew interpretation of that verse actually reads this way, "God promised Abraham, "I will make you into a great nation and I will bless you; I will make your name great, and you will be a blessing. I will bless those who bless you and whoever *lightly esteems or ignores* you I will *bitterly curse*; and all the peoples on the earth will be blessed through you."

Wow, that is quite a different translation than I had been taught in church. If this verse is true, and it is, because Yahweh doe not lie, it explains why we have not seen the fullness of the blessings of Yahweh in the Christian church.

The revelation of the understanding of why we must humble ourselves and partner with the Jewish people does not rely on an understanding of Israel. It relies on an understanding of Yahweh's sovereignty and His right to choose a people. It is about the Protocol of Yahweh.

Arni Klein says, "The literal Hebrew actually says, I will curse bitterly those who lightly esteem you. The peoples of the earth are under a curse, out of ignorance.. If you don't take Israel to heart, you are under a curse. There is a curse where something is cast down on you, but then there is a curse where something is withheld."

He continues, "There are nations that are under Yahweh's bitter curse because they have stood against Yahweh's protocol, Yahweh's strategic plan, and Yahweh's determined, decreed authority. And there are those who are walking around on half power because they've not lined up with the plan...their heart is right, and they want to do the right thing, but they haven't clicked into how Yahweh says, 'This is the way it works. I built it like this.'"

In Don Finto's book, *Your People Shall Be My People*, he says, "If this ancient promise that was made to Abraham is still true, and it is, then no person, no congregation, no nation, or people group will ever receive their fullest blessing until they learn to love the Jewish people."[1]

Have you ever wondered why there is so much fuss over a little piece of land in the Middle East? The problem is not really about land and it is not really about people. It is about Yahweh's right to choose. Suuqiina says, " If Yahweh had chosen the Inuit people of Alaska, everyone would be fighting over Alaska. It is about Yahweh's right to choose."

"Jews have been expelled from nearly every country in which they have resided. They have been beaten, tortured, and murdered, all for one reason, because they were Jews. The Jews have been hated from generation to generation."[2] Look at this evidence:

135AD - Romans prohibit (upon pain of death) circumcision, reading the Torah, eating unleavened bread during Passover, and other required Jewish rituals

200AD - The Roman Emperor Severus prohibits conversion to Judaism upon penalty of death.

306AD - Roman law prohibits Jews and Christians from eating together, intermarrying, or having sexual relations

489AD - Citizens of Antioch slaughter Jews, burn the synagogue, and throw the bodies of Jewish people into the fire.

681AD - The Synod of Toledo mandates to burn the Talmud and other Jewish texts

855AD - Louis II expels Jews from Italy

1021AD - A group of Jews in Rome are arrested, accused of causing an earthquake and hurricane by tormenting a "host" (the water used in mass). They are burned to death after confessing under torture.

1099AD - The First Crusaders arrive in Palestine, slaughter 30,000 Muslims and Jews. Jerusalem Jews are gathered in the synagogue and burned alive.

1180AD - The King of France, Philip Augustus, seizes all Jewish property and expels Jews from the country.

1290AD - Jews are expelled from England.

1306AD - Jews are expelled from France.

1349AD - Jews throughout Europe are massacred: the entire Jewish community of Basle is burned to death; 6,000 Jews are burned to death in Mainz; 500 Jews are killed in Brussels; Jews in Frankfurt and Vienna commit suicide to avoid torture.

1391AD - Ten of thousands of Jews are killed in anti-Jewish riots in Spain, tens of thousands more are saved by forced conversion; the Inquisition begins, during which 50,000 Jews are killed.

1492AD - Jews are expelled from Spain.

1517AD - The Pope declares all Jews must wear badges of shame and live in ghettos.

1543AD - Martin Luther, founder of the Protestant Reformation, declares that the Jews, "synagogues should be set on fire...their houses should likewise be broken down and destroyed...their rabbis must be forbidden under the threat of death to teach..."

1648AD - The Chmelnitski Pogroms occur; 100,000 to 200,000 Jews are killed in the Ukraine.

1862AD - General Ulysses Grant orders all Jews to be expelled from Tennessee (an order almost immediately rescinded by President Abraham Lincoln).

1894AD - Alfred Dreyfus, an assimilated Jew, is falsely accused of espionage in France.

1900-1920AD - Thousands of Jews are killed in pogroms across Eastern Europe

1915AD- Russia forcibly moves 600,000 Jews from the Western border to the interior; over 100,000 die of exposure or starvation.

1925AD- Adolph Hitler publishes *Mein Kampf*, in which he writes, "Today I believe that I am acting in accordance with the will of the Almighty Creator; by defending myself against the Jew, I am fighting for the work of the Lord."

1941-45AD- The Holocaust. Almost six million Jews (including 1.5 million children) are killed in death camps."[3]

Pretty overwhelming statistics I would say. Why all this hatred for the Jews? Might it be because Satan knows what we, as Christians, have not discovered? That being, the promises of Yahweh will not be fulfilled if Israel is destroyed.

Earlier this year, Suuqina and I came upon a document of which most Jews know about, but the average Christian is ignorant. It is called *Constantine's Christian Creed* and was adopted at the Council of Nicea around 325AD by our early church fathers. In light of the promise that Yahweh made to Abraham, the document sent shudders up our spines. It reads:

"I renounce all customs, rites, legalisms, unleavened breads, and sacrifices of lambs of the Hebrews, and all the other feasts of the Hebrews, sacrifices, prayers, aspirations, purifications, sanctifications, and propitiations, and fasts, and new moons, amd Sabbaths, and superstitions, and hymns and chants, and observances and synagogues and the food and the drink of the Hebrews;

The Protocol of Elohim Concerning Israel

I renounce absolutely everything Jewish, every law, rite and custom and if afterward I shall wish to deny and return to Jewish superstition, or shal be found eating with Jews, or feasting with them, or secretly conversing and condemning the Christian religion instead of openly confuting them and condeming their vain faith, then let the trembling of Cain, and the leprosy of Gehazi cleave to me, as well as the legal punishments to which I acknowledge myself liable.

And may I be an anathema in the world to come, and may my soul be set down with Satan and the devils.

I accept all customs, rites, legalisms, and feasts of the Romans, sacrifices, prayers, purifications with water, sanctifications by the Pontificus Maxmus, propitiations, and feasts, and the new Sabbath "Sol dei (Sunday- Day of the Sun), and new chants and observances, and all the food and drinks of the Romans.

I accept everything Roman, every new law, rite, and custom of Rome, and *the new Roman Religion.*"[4]

I don't know about you, but I never signed up for a new Roman Religion. I never signed up for one but I have been affected by it, and by this document that these forefathers in the Christian church initiated, endorsed, and enforced many years ago.

Please consider the facts and implications of this creed. Three hundred eighteen Bishops of the church met and overthrew our Hebrew history and pulled themselves out of the root of the tree in which the "gathered out ones" were grafted (see Romans 11). A new plant was planted called the *New Roman*

Religion and a far-reaching system of religion and worship was established that spread throughout the whole world. This new "man inspired" plant has affected every generation since 325AD. The early "gathered out ones" had kept Yahweh's Sabbaths and His Feasts (They are called the Feasts of the Lord not the Feasts of the Jews). They had demonstrated the "One New Man" of Ephesians two until this Council.

Ask yourself this question, "Was this document inspired by the Holy Spirit?

In light of these scriptures from *Our Hands Are Stained With Blood*, a book by Michael Brown, how could it have been? (Emphasis added)

> Brothers, my heart's desire and prayer to God for the *Israelites* is that they may be saved. (Romans 10:1)

Which *Israelites* did Paul Mean? The Natural children!

> Again I ask: Did *Israel* not understand?...concerning *Israel* He says, "All day long I have held out my hands to a dis - obedient and obstinate people." (Romans 10:19-21)

Which *Israel* did Paul mean? The natural children.

> I ask then: Did God reject His people? By no means! I am an *Israelite* myself, a descendant of Abraham, from the tribe of Benjamin. God did not reject His people, whom He foreknew...." (Romans 11:1-2)

Which *Israelites* did Paul mean? The natural children.

The Protocol of Elohim Concerning Israel

*...Don't you know what the Scripture says in the passage about Elijah—how he appealed to God for **Israel**."* (Romans 11:2)

Which *Israel* did Paul mean? The natural children.

*What then? What **Israel** sought so earnestly it did not obtain, but the elect did. The others were hardened.* (Romans 11:7)

Which *Israel* did Paul mean? The natural children.

*Again I ask: "Did they (Israel) stumble so as to fall beyond recovery? Not at all! (Let the church repeat these words out loud: **Israel** did not stumble beyond recovery.) Rather, because of their transgression, salvation has come to the Gentiles to make **Israel** envious."* (Romans 11:11)

Which Israel is Paul talking about? The natural children. Paul is talking to the gentiles here **about** *Israel*. He is not telling them that **they are** Israel.

*I do not want you to be ignorant of this mystery, brothers, so that you may not be conceited: **Israel** has experienced a hardening in part until the fullness of the Gentiles has come in.* (Romans 11:25)

Which *Israel* is Paul talking about? The natural children.

*And so all **Israel** will be saved...* (Romans 11:26-27)

Which *Israel* did Paul mean? The natural children."[5]

Because Israel was hardened in part, we as gentiles, are able to be grafted into the olive tree of which the Book of Romans speaks. Yes Israel fell away, but the scriptures say, "He will take away their sins." They will receive the same mercy that we have received.

We are warned in Romans 11:17-18 to not fall into pride and arrogance concerning His people, the Jews, and concerning the fact that we are now in the tree.

> *If some of the (natural Israelite) branches have been broken off, and you (Gentiles), though a wild olive shoot, have been grafted in among the others (the Israelites who believed) and now share in the nourishing sap from the olive root. (Israel),* **do not boast** *over those branches. If you do, con - sider this: you do not support the root, but the root supports you. (Romans 11:17-18)*

Paul was speaking prophetically to the church in Rome, that would later (325AD) lead the way in drafting a document that would renounce the root and pull themselves out from the planting of the Lord. Their actions spoke for them, "I know what you said, Yahweh, but we are going to do it our way."

Was Constantine's Christian Creed inspired by the Holy Spirit? Line it up with scripture. I think not!

Romans 11 makes it perfectly clear that Gentile believers in Yeshua have been grafted into Israel's tree, and we are nourished by the ancient Jewish root. We were admonished not to boast over the fallen Israelite branches. Instead, we have treated the Jews harshly. Many times the church has been the source of their abuse and torture. Many people who did not participate in their persecution, turned their heads, refus- ing to associate with the Jews or identify with their suffering.

Don Finto tells a story about a trip in which he and a group of believers experienced a stark reminder of the crimes committed against the Jews, all in the name of Christianity.

"Recently while in Spain with a friendship group of Jews and Gentiles, I visited historical sites of anti-Jewish legislation and persecution in former years. In Granada we stood in the Ambassador Room of Alhambra Palace, where Ferdinand and Isabella had signed the 1492 decree to evict Jews and confiscate their property. Here we were revisiting events, confessing sins and asking for forgiveness on behalf of ancestors long dead, whose decisions continues to affect us to this day.

These were very emotional gatherings, but nothing had prepared us for what we would see when, in Toledo, we rounded the corner of an ancient street and came upon Suan Juan de los Reyes. Hanging from the walls of this old monastery were the chains with which Jewish people had been tortured and killed five centuries earlier- stark reminders of a dark past. This was not an abandoned building. Grains of rice were strewn on the cobblestones outside the cathedral, where a bridal party had been celebrating earlier that day.

Why were the chains still hanging there" Why had they not been removed? Our small band was struck dumb. Embarrassed, ashamed and stunned, we bowed our heads and backed away. And yet in the throes of grief and shame, I remember a kind of numbness in my heart as if there were no way to emote deeply enough to express what ought to be felt at such a time.

Around the corner was a small park. We shuffled toward the area and huddled together, still in speechless consternation. Then one of our Jewish mothers sat down on the ground and began to throw dust on her head, her way of expressing the inexpressible. I sat beside her, following her lead. Others, Jew and Gentile, held each other. After a long season of silence, someone began saying Kaddish- the Jewish prayer for the dead- honoring the Jewish men, women, and children who had been tormented and murdered by past generations of "Christians."

Don continues, "Back in the first century, the Jews had graciously received us as equals in the family. But we had rejected them. Paul, the apostle to the Gentiles, had begun to see the danger signs in the last days of his life. "Do not boast over those branches," he had warned the Romans. "If you do, consider this: You do not support the root, but the root supports you. Do not be arrogant." (Romans 11:18-20) But arrogant we have been! Paul's admonition has gone unheeded for almost 20 centuries!"[6]

Here is more history that you might not know. When Jewish people converted to Catholicism they were required to say words similar to these:

"I do here and now renounce every rite and observance of the Jewish religion, detesting all it's most solemn ceremonies and tenets that in former days I kept and held. In the future I will practice no rite or celebration connected with it, nor any custom of my past error, promising neither to seek it out or perform it...I promise that I will never return to the vomit of Jewish superstition. Never again will I fulfill any of the offices of Jewish ceremonies to which I was addicted, nor ever more hold them dear. (I will) shun all intercourse with other Jews and have the circle of my friends only among other Christians.

We will not associate with the accursed Jews who remain unbaptized. We will not practice carnal circumcision, or celebrate the Passover, The Sabbath or the other feast days connected with the Jewish religion. With regard to swine's flesh we promise to observe this rule, that if through long custom we are hardly able to eat it, we shall not through fastidiousness or error refuse the things that are cooked with it. And if in all the matters touched on above we are found in any was to transgress (then) whoever of us is found to transgress shall either perish by the hands of our fellows, by burning or stoning, or (if our lives are spared), we shall at once lose our liberty and you shall give us along with all our property to whomever you please into perpetual slavery.

I renounce the whole worship of the Hebrews, circumcision, and all it's legalisms, unleavened bread, Passover, the sacrificing of lambs, the feasts of Weeks, Jubilees, Trumpets Atonement, Tabernacles, and all other Hebrew feasts, their sacrifices, prayers, aspirations, purifications, expiations, fasts, Sabbaths, new moons, food and drinks. And I absolutely renounce every custom and institution of the Jewish laws...in one word, I renounce absolutely everything Jewish.

Together with the ancients, I anathamatise also the Chief Rabbis and new evil doctors of the Jews. And I believe and profess the Blessed Virgin Mary, who bore Him according to the flesh, and who remained a virgin, to be truly and actually the Mother of God, and I venerate and honour her truly as the Mother of God Incarnate, and as the Lady and mistress of all creation.

If I wander from the straight path in any way and defile the holy Faith, and try to observe any rites of the Jewish sect, or if I shall delude you in any way in swearing of this oath…then may all the curses of the law fall upon me…May there fall upon me and upon my house and all my children all the plagues that smote Egypt, and to the horror of others may I suffer in addition the fate of Dathan and Abiram, so that the earth shall swallow me alive, and after I am deprived of this life I shall be handed over to the eternal fire, in the company of the Devil and his Angels, sharing with the dwellers in Sodom and with Judas the punishment of burning; and when I arrive before the tribunal of the fearful and glorious Judge, our Lord Jesus Christ, may I be numbered in that company to whom the glorious and terrible Judge with threatening men will say, "Depart from Me, evil-doers, into the eternal fire that is prepared for the Devil and his angels."[7]

An example of the hatred for the Jews is reflected in the life of Saint John Chrysostom. He was described as, "A bright, cheerful, gentle soul, a sensitive heart, a temperament open to emotion and impulse." He was known as one of the most eloquent preachers of truth and love. This man was esteemed as one of the greatest of the "Church Fathers." And yet this is how Chrysostom spoke of the Jewish people:

"The synagogue is worse than a brothel...it is the den of scoundrels and the repair of wild beasts...the temple of demons devoted to idolatrous cults...the refuge of brigands and debauchees, and the cavern of devils. (It is) a criminal assembly of Jews...a place of meeting for the assassins of Christ...a house worse than a drinking shop...a den of thieves; a house of ill fame, a dwelling of iniquity, the refuge of devils, a gulf and abyss of perdition."[8]

It is hard to believe that these are the statements of men that the church revered.

But you might say, "That does not apply to the foundation of my faith because it is not Catholic," Let's hear what Martin Luther, the father of the Protestant faith had to say concerning the Jews.

"First their synagogues should be set on fire...Secondly, their homes should likewise be broken down and destroyed...Thirdly, they should be deprived of their prayer books and Talmuds...Fourthly, their rabbis must be forbidden under threat of death to teach any more...Fifthly, passport and traveling privileges should be absolutely forbidden to the Jews...Sixthly, they ought to be stopped from usury (charging interest on loans) Seventhly, let the young and strong Jews and Jewesses be given the flail, the ax, the how, the spade, the distaff, and spindle, and let them earn their bread by the sweat of their noses...We ought to drive the rascally lazy bones out of our system...Therefore away with them.... To sum up, dear princess and nobles who have Jews in your domains, if this advice of mine does not suit you, then find a better one so that you and we may all be free of the insufferable devilish burden...the Jews."[9]

These despicable words fanned the fires in the ovens of the death camps during the holocaust. Hitler quotes Luther in Hitler's classic work *Mein Kampf*. Hitler and the Nazis reprinted Martin Luther's anti-Semitic writings and used them to build a unjust case against the Jews. One of Hitler's generals, Albert Spier, was quoted at the Nuremberg trials as saying, "I only did what Martin Luther spoke of." As millions of Jews were carried off to death camps, the so-called Christian church, for the most part stood by and did nothing. In one town, while they loaded crying Jews onto the box cars, the Christians in the church service nearby sang their hymns louder, to drown out the cries of the Jews. Yahweh have mercy on us.

Yahweh instructed us to make Israel jealous or envious. Were we obedient to this commission? No we were not. Instead of making them jealous, we have had this affect on them as shown in these writings by an Israeli.

He says, "Instead of bringing redemption to the Jews, the false Christian messiah has brought down on us base libels and expulsions, oppressive restrictions and burning of our holy books, devastations and destructions. Christianity, which professes to infuse the sick world with love and compassion, has fixed a course directly opposed to this lofty rhetoric. The voice of the blood of millions of our brothers cries out to us from the ground: "No! Christianity is not a religion of love but a religion of unfathomable hate! All history, from ancient times to our own day, is one continuous proof of the total bankruptcy of this religion and all its segments."[10]

So now we look back and see the huge mess that we are in even after we were warned by Paul to not be proud and arrogant, but prideful and arrogant we have been.

"We not only have stolen the birthright of Yahweh's first born, Israel, through our vain attempts to 'run the show,' we have heaped upon ourselves a curse."

We not only have stolen the birthright of Yahweh's first born, Israel, through our vain attempts to "run the show," we have heaped upon ourselves a curse. Remember "those who lightly esteem and ignore you I will bitterly curse (see Gen. 12:3)."

We have sown to the wind, in the way that we have dealt treacherously with our elder brother, and unless we repent and turn from our ways, we will reap the whirlwind.

"The church split happened in 325 AD at the Council of Nicea. We split away from our Jewish roots and the church has been splitting ever since. We continue to have division because we have sown it. We will continue to have division until we admit what we have done and return to Yahweh's sovereign plan for us."[11]

Obadiah 1:10-15 clearly shows us the consequences of dealing harshly with the Jews. It reads, "Because of the violence against your brother Jacob, you will be covered with shame; you will be destroyed forever. On the day you stood aloof while strangers carried off his wealth and foreigners entered his gates and cast lots for Jerusalem, you were like one of them. You should not look down on your brother in the day of his misfortune...nor boast so much in the day of their trouble...The day of the Lord is near all nations. As you have done, it will be done to you; your deeds will return upon your own head."

Yahweh, please have mercy on us!

So, what are we to do in this late hour? How can we be people of honor and what can we do to protocol a people that have been so offended and wounded by our "faith?" One word...Humility.

First we must repent. Repent for what our forefathers have done in ignorance and willful disobedience. We cannot say I am not responsible. The former offenders are not present and it is up to our generation to make restitution and work toward restoration. We have been given the ministry of reconciliation and we are spiritual representatives empowered to do the necessary repair work.

We can also renounce these anti-Semitic documents, creeds, and statements that the founding fathers of the church have made. We must not make excuses for this unacceptable behavior in the guise of respecting our ancestors.

We must ask Yahweh to cleanse us of anti-Semitism. We cannot say, "Am I anti-Semitic?" We must ask, "**How** anti-Semitic am I?" We have been a part of a religious system that has been steeped in anti-Semitism and we have been affected.

We must be aware that the world and its media are prejudiced in regards to Yahweh and His people.

We are supposed to provoke them to jealousy. There is not a greater way to do this than through serving them, without preaching. Another way is to learn about their culture and their customs by educating oneself on the Shabbat, the Feasts of the Lord, and the Torah. They have awesome and profound insights to give to us if we will be teachable and willing to learn from them.

We are to show them mercy and compassion. We can begin by hearing their stories. We can absorb the pain of their hearts through the simple act of listening, without lecturing and proselytizing. Don Finto says in His book, *Your People Shall Be My People*, "If there were never to be another Jewish person in history who believes in Jesus as Messiah, we must still be committed to them as friends, brothers/sisters, protectors."[12]

We must not judge them or their faith as less than ours and we must repent of being condescending. We must pray for them and keep in contact with them through email, phone, and over meals.

"We must partner with them on a regular basis. It must not be with a paternalistic approach where we "help" them by running the show. It must be with humility, inviting them to speak in to our personal lives, and the life of our churches and city. Since they are the "elder brother," we are to respect them as co-leaders, when we plan our conferences and meetings. We can show our good intentions, toward equal partnership and leadership, by calling them to the table of the Lord during planning sessions, to carry out the vision of Yahweh instead of using them as "token" Jews."[13]

We can bless then financially. The scriptures say, "Where your treasure is there your heart will be also." We are instructed to bless Israel as an act of obedience. The financial support will also remind them that they are not alone and that we stand with them in every sense of the word.

We must prepare, now, to come to the aid of the Jews in the future. That future may well be nigh

"We must prepare, now, to come to the aid of the Jews in the future."

upon us. As we travel the globe, we are aware that Yahweh is calling His people to establish places of refuge for the Jewish people. People are building safe houses, storing food, and purchasing vehicles for the next great Exodus. These people, who are preparing are not conspiracy theorists. They are children of the King, like Esther, who have their ears to His heart. They know the time will come swiftly and that we must be prepared.

We can help the Jewish people, financially, to return to their land, the land of Israel. We can encourage them to do so. Persecution is increasing word-wide toward the Jews, even in America. Although the battle in Israel is great, very soon, the safest place for them to be is in the land that Yahweh established for them, the land of Israel. It will better for them to leave now and become established in the land, before the next great shaking is upon us all.

We can help them be released into their calling and anointing. The prophetic destiny of Israel is to be a light to the nations. "Although the whole earth is mine, you will be for me a kingdom of priests and a holy nation," Yahweh said to Moses as He led the Israelites through the desert out of Egyptian bondage (Exodus 19:5-6). Israel was then and is now to represent Yahweh to the nations until "all the ends of the earth will see the salvation of our God."(Isaiah 52:10) "For the

Lord has commanded us: I have set you to be a light to the Gentiles, that you should be for salvation to the ends of the earth (Acts 13:47)." They were to be and are to be a whole nation of worshippers.

Because we have been cut off, for generations, from our Jewish heritage, we have lost much prophetic understanding of the scriptures. It was not until I had come to terms with the Jewish root of my faith, that I could understand the scriptures concerning Ruth and how they point to the Gentile/Jewish relationship.

(Please read the Book of Ruth) Naomi, a Hebrew, is the mother-in-law of Orpah and Ruth. She is a prophetic picture of the nation of Israel, who is dispersed to the nations, due to spiritual famine and drought. The husband of Naomi and her sons have died and she is left alone with her two daughters-in-law. Orpha, whose name means, "The Back of One's Neck," and Ruth, whose name means "Friend and Comrade," prophetically represent two types of believers. One type will turn its back on Israel and the other type will be her friend.

Although both women, or types, professed their love for Naomi (Israel) and cried tears, Orpah turned and left while Ruth clung to her mother-in-law.

Ruth says, "Do not urge me to leave you or turn back from following you; for where you go, I will go, and where you lodge, I will lodge. Your people will be my people, and your Elohim, my Elohim." As she clung to the people (Israel) she could therefore cling to their Elohim, the Elohim of Abraham, Isaac, and Jacob.

As Naomi reenters her land, she tells her people to no longer call her Naomi (the name means "Pleasant") but to call her Mara (the name means "Bitter"). She says, "Do not call me Naomi; call me Mara, for the Almighty has dealt bitterly with me...(Ruth 1:20). This is the picture of Israel that we see today. The land and the people have been afflicted and continue to be hard pressed on every side.

As the story progresses, Ruth is instructed, by Naomi, to glean in the fields of Boaz (his name means "In Him There Is Strength"). He was the kinsmen-redeemer, who had the legal right to redeem the name and property of the deceased (Naomi's husband and sons). Ruth caught the attention of Boaz because her servants heart toward her mother-in-law. "All that you have done for your mother-in-law after the death of your husband has been fully reported to me" (Ruth 2:11).

Ruth captures the heart of Boaz and she becomes his bride, she conceives and bears him a son. And though she had been married before and had no children, the Lord opened her womb, for this appointed time, to bear a son.

And yet the scriptures read, "A son has been born to Naomi!" (Ruth 4:17) Ruth laid her child in the lap of her mother-in-law and Naomi became a nurse to him. Ruth, a gentile, was used to restore the generational line that brought us our Messiah. The son of Ruth and Boaz was Obed, the father of Jesse, who was the father of King David. Yes, Yahweh used a gentile to preserve the remnant of Israel through a grafting process. He made the two, one, through Ruth and Boaz and this act was a foreshadowing of the Jew and Gentile people uniting through another son, the Son of our Elohim.

Ruth (the gentile church) did not replace Boaz (the Jew), but joined him. She became intimately united with him and gave birth through him and with him. His Yahweh and the

Yahweh of Naomi had become her Yahweh. She was a citizen of their land and a receiver of the promises that had been made to Abraham, Isaac and Jacob."[14]

Which one are you, a Ruth or an Orpah? We have entered the age that was prophesied when Naomi would once again re-enter her land. Will we leave her in her hour of need or, will we cleave to her, and in so doing, help her to give birth to her prophetic destiny. That destiny, to be a light to the nations, and to be a nation of worshippers, is still in the balance. Hear the cries of Israel,

"Ruth (the gentile church) did not replace Boaz (the Jew), but joined him."

૪ટ

"We were pregnant, we writhed in labor, we gave birth, as it were, only to wind. We could not accomplish deliverance for the earth nor were inhabitants of the world born (Isaiah 26:18)." It is not too late, now is the time!

While in Hawaii, at the World Christian Gathering On Indigenous People, Arni Klein shared with us a revelation that He was given. It gave clarity to us of the importance of the people groups of the world recovering their cultural expressions in worship to offer to Yeshua.

Arni opened this scripture to us, "For I do not desire, brethren, that you should be ignorant of this mystery, lest you should be wise in your own opinion, that hardening in part has happened to Israel until the fullness of the Gentiles has come in. And so all Israel will be saved, as it is written: The Deliverer will come out of Zion, And He will turn away ungodliness from Jacob; For this is My covenant with them, when I take away their sins (Romans 11:25-26)."

Arni told us that the meaning for the word gentiles here is "ethnos" (Grk. Ta ethnae), it means ethnic groups. When the ethnic groups come into their fullness or better said, when they are restored to their ethnicity, then "all Israel will be saved." We are in the time in history when the indigenous peoples of the world are recovering their cultures for the purpose of worshipping the Lord. We native peoples are not recovering our regalia, languages and instruments for the sole purposes of our own fulfillment. It is so that we might make Israel envious, that we are worshipping their Yahweh and their Jewish Messiah, in all the splendor that the Creator endowed us.

The Gentile coming into fulfillment is where we are now in history. We have yet to see all Israel being saved, but we are at threshold of the door. Why does all Israel need to be saved for the Kingdom of Yahweh to be established on the earth? Protocol. One simple word sums it up. Yahweh set it up that way. The native soul understands protocol. The native soul understands honor and obedience to the Chief, Chief Cornerstone, Yeshua, gives us a clue in the scriptures.

Remember in the chapter titled "Entering Another Nation," we talked about the protocol of entering someone's land? Yeshua was from the Galilee area, from Nazareth. When he entered Jerusalem for the Feast, the people welcomed him onto the land with a protocol ceremony worthy of a King.

The next day a great multitude that had come to the feast, when they heard that Yeshua was coming to Jerusalem, took branches of palm trees and went out to meet Him and cried out: Hosanna! Blessed is He who comes in the name of the Lord! The King of Israel! (John 12:12)

The Protocol of Elohim Concerning Israel

Protocol was observed in this ceremony and, some day, in the future, it will be observed again when He returns to His land as King of Kings. He will not return until *His people*, the *Jewish* people, the people of *His culture*, **call Him back!**

> *On that very day some of the Pharisees came, saying to Him, "Get out and depart from here, for Herod wants to kill You." And He said to them, "Go and tell that fox, Behold I cast out demons and perform cures today and tomorrow, and the third day I shall be perfected. Nevertheless I must journey today, tomorrow, and the day following; for it cannot be that a prophet should perish outside of Jerusalem. Oh Jerusalem, Jerusalem, the one who kills the prophets and stones those who are sent to her! How often I wanted to gather your children together, as a hen gathers her brood under her wings, but you were not willing! See! Your house is left to you desolate and assuredly, I say to you, you shall not see Me until the **time comes** when YOU say, 'Blessed is He who comes in the name of the Lord!'"* (Luke 13:31-35, emphasis added)

He set up the protocol and now we will follow it. He is Yahweh and it is His right to choose.

So there it is. We can get with His program or beat the air. Will we be grafted in so that we can be a part of the commonwealth of Israel? If we are adopted sons of Abraham should we not know of our adopted culture? "The Feasts of the Lord are forever," the scriptures say. Would it not be to our benefit to have some understanding of them. Yeshua kept the Sabbath and the Feasts, the scriptures say. Might we not benefit from participating in them as well?

I want everything that Christ afforded me in this new life. I want to know Him and His people, and I want the inheritance that is mine through Father Abraham and His lineage.

Some might say, "Israel, the Jewish people, that doesn't fit into my theology."

I will leave you with a story.

The story is about Allie Nicole, our grandaughter. Allie was two years old when we raised the Israeli flag on our land, with Arni and Yonit Klein from Tel Aviv Israel. All the grandchildren were gathered around the flag pole and the Kleins laid hands on them and gave them a blessing prayer from Zion. All the children were there except Allie. She was asleep, inside the house of her mother and father, taking her nap. Her mother, Kimberly, exclaimed to me, at the conclusion of the blessing, "I forgot to go get Allie so that she could be a part of the prayer of blessing." I answered, "When she gets up from her nap we will have the Kleins pray for her."

That is exactly what happened. We went inside the house, for a great spread of food and fellowship, and as soon as she woke up, Arni and Yonit prayed a blessing over her.

Six weeks later, as the flag flew over our land, Allie slipped from the house, for a brief moment in time, and drowned in our back yard pool. We were devastated and the grief was so heavy. For many days it felt like we were drowning ourselves, it was so hard to breathe. Yahweh provided incredible grace, but that did not erase the pain of our loss. The night of Allie's death, as I was helping her mother, Kimberly into the bed, Kimberly said to me, "This scripture keeps running through my head, "A voice is heard in Ramah, lamentation and bitter weeping. Rachel is weeping for her children; she refuses to be comforted for her children are no more (Jeremiah 31)."

She continued, "That is how I feel. There is no comfort for me." The room that I stayed in was underneath Kimberly's room, and all night, as I sat on my bed, I heard her groaning and weeping for Allie, her child.

The funeral for Allie was memorable. The Lord provided grace for Allie's parents and myself to do the eulogy for Allie, and we all celebrated memories of her life and shared the hope in Yeshua that we would be with her again.

Weeks went by and we were left with the very real pain of building a life without Allie in our midst. Some days were better than others but we were sustained by our Savior.

During the weeks that passed, Kimberly would often say to me, "I know that I have the Israel flag on my land and I know that it must mean something. I know I must have a connection to Israel, but I don't *feel* an emotional connection to Israel. I am sowing into Israel and blessing Israel out of obedience because He tells me to do so." I encouraged her that she did not have to feel anything. Abba would honor her obedience.

A few months later, at a Hanukkah gathering, I noticed that Kimberly was sitting off to herself and she was crying. I walked over to her and asked her if she was o.k. She assured me that she was allright and then she began to share.

She said, "The Lord just spoke to me and told me what my connection is to Israel." I asked her if she could share it with me and she said she could. This is what she said, "Do you remember when Allie died and the people from the churches gave us money and we were so glad to have the support but it felt weird to have money in place of Allie?" I nodded yes. "Do you remember when Allie died and the people from the churches gave us memorial trees to plant in our yard and as we watched them plant them it felt strange to have a tree in place of Allie?" Once again I nodded yes. "Do you remember when Allie died and the people from the churches gave us statues and figurines of little girls and it felt strange to have a statue in place of Allie?" I nodded yes.

> *"To Yahweh, it is not about theology, it is about relationship."*

"Well, the Lord just spoke to me and told me this, 'I don't need my people's offerings of money, and I don't need their plantings in ministry, and I don't need their statues and buildings that they erect for me. I just want my child back. Israel, my first born child."

She looked at me and, as the tears rolled down her face, she said, "With the loss of Allie, I bare the heart-pain of the Lord for Israel in my own heart." Kimberly learned a valuable lesson that day. This is not about Israel, it is about Yahweh's heart.

With her words, I was immediately taken back to the night of Allie's death. I remembered that night that Kimberly shared the scripture of Rachel weeping for her children and refusing to be comforted "because they were no more." I remembered sitting on my bed listening to her moan and groan for her child. So, this is how the Father feels for Israel? He is moaning and groaning with grief, and He refuses to be comforted until they are reunited with Him.

It was Moses who first heard Yahweh say, "Israel is my first-born son (Exodus 4:22)." Kimberly heard those words again that day…"Israel my first born son."

The Protocol of Elohim Concerning Israel

To Yahweh, it is not about theology, it is about relationship. It is not about religion, it is about relationship. It is not about denominational doctrines, it is about relationship. It is about a family, His family. It is about a Father's heart for His children.

After Kimberly shared her words, Yahweh spoke to my grandmother's heart about Allie and He said this to me, "And so shall it be...just as the day you raised the Israel flag on your land, and Allie was in her fathers house sleeping, you will continue the work with Israel on the land and later at the end of the age, you will join Allie at a great feast in the house of her/your Father where you we will be together for eternity."

We have laid our treasure, Allie Nicole, in heaven with the Father and we will labor to see that His treasure, Israel, His first born son, will join us at the great feast in our Father's house.

> *"Someday in the future the whole world will take a*
> *stand against Israel. Then our earthly nationality will no*
> *longer be important. All that will matter is that we are*
> *born-again-into-the-Kingdom, fellow citizens with Israel."*[15]
>
> —Don Finto

*For behold, in those days and at that time, when I bring back the captives of Judah and Jerusalem, I will also gather **all nations**, and bring them down to the Valley of Jehoshaphat; and I will **enter into judgement with them** there **on account of My people, My heritage Israel**, whom they have scattered among the nations. **They have also divided up My land.** Joel 3:1-2*

Warfare by Honor

Chapter Fourteen

The Practice of Protocol Through Restorative Acts

Now all things are of Yahweh, who has reconciled us to Himself through Yeshua Hamachiach, and has given us the ministry of reconciliation. 2 Corinthians 5: 18

In 1999, we were privileged to speak in an Episcopal Church in California. It was our first time to meet with them and as usual we did protocol. We gifted them and asked them to welcome us on to the land of their church home. We humbled ourselves and asked them to release to us the authority to impart what Yahweh had placed on our hearts.

The Priest and his wife were moved to implement protocol in their area of the city. They asked each other, "Where should we start?" They answered with, "I guess we should where Yahweh started ...with the Jews."

Father C.* called the Reform Jewish Temple in his city and spoke to the Rabbi. He said, "We are the Episcopal Church in your area and we would like to bring our people to come and bless you." I believe that the Rabbi made some sort of remark like, "We are the Jewish people, we have the blessing." Father C. responded with, "We want to come and repent to you, the Jewish people, for what Christians have done, negatively, to your people and we want to submit to you as our elder broth- er because we are grafted into you." The Rabbi said, "You can come."

Father C. and his wife S. and their church went to the Jewish Synagogue and did just that. They repented for what had happened to the Jewish people historically and the Jewish people were moved. Father C. then went a step further than most reconciliation meetings have done in the past. He explained to the Jewish congregation that the Episcopal Church members were not looking for a one-time ceremony. They were looking for a relationship with these wonderful Jewish people. They asked if they could partner with this syn- agogue and spend time with them. This is exactly what they did. One extra small step of humility has made the difference in a one-time feels-good ceremony versus a long time com- mitted relationship in the Kingdom of Yahweh.

The men at the Episcopal Church went out and bought kippas to wear on their heads at the Friday night Shabbat service. They wore them to honor the Jewish people. They sat in on the all-Hebrew service, where they didn't understand a word, in order to be near to Yahweh's first-born child, His Hebrew children.

Father C. went out to eat lunch regularly with the Rabbi and they shared their faiths with one another in mutual respect and were willing to learn from one another.

In one such meeting the Rabbi told Father C. that the High Holy days were approaching and that the Jewish members would have to rent space for their celebration, because their synagogue was too small to accommodate the people that would come out for the services. Father C. said, "You don't have to rent space. You can use our church building. We will cover up all the crosses so that your people will not be offended." The Rabbi took Father C. up on his offer and they celebrated the High Holy Days as guests in the Episcopal Church.

One day Father C. told the Rabbi that we were coming to town, and that he would love to introduce him to us. He said, "You need to meet the First Nations people. They are the ones who taught us about protocol. It is a real blessing to be welcomed on the land by the host people of the land." Of course the Rabbi, being of Jacob's seed, did not hesitate to reach out to get the blessing. He said, " We would like to have these First Nations people come and speak to our synagogue."

When we heard about the invitation, we prayed, "Oh Father, let us not offend these precious people by speaking "Christian-ese. Let us be a light and let us honor your chosen people." To some this might sound like we were not standing up as Christians. That is so far from the truth. We wanted to carry Yeshua in our hearts and build a relationship with these people. It is difficult to build a relationship with someone who is offended, so we purposed not to offend them in any way, but simply to honor them.

We started with protocol by gifting the Rabbi and his wife with two Star of David medallions, hand carved by a Jewish holocaust survivor from Israel. Then Suuqiina told the congregation about the trip to Israel when 96 First Nation's People met with Avram Burg, the President of the Knesset. He shared of the bond that the indigenous people have with the Jews.

Qaumaniq said, "We are here to honor you tonight as the apple of God's eye. He loves you so much and we know that He has chosen you to lead in the role call of nations. We are so grateful to you because you brought us the Torah, His word. We would not have it if you had not brought it to us. You are the ones that He kept with His shekinah glory in the wilderness. He tells us that if we bless you, we will be blessed and that, if we lightly esteem or ignore you, we will be bitterly cursed. He has made a treaty with you and He is not a treaty breaker. We are to honor you because He said to in His word. He also said that your prophetic destiny is to be a light to the nations and we are drawn to His light that He has placed in you. You are our elder brother and we are grafted into you."

We sat down and the Rabbi came up and stood behind the scrolls. He said, "Well, I am now convinced that the Torah is not just for our people but for all nations. Children you may now gather under the talit (as is their tradition) and Suuqiina and Qaumaniq would you please lay hands on our children and bless them." What an honor to be asked to bless the Jewish children.

Another added blessing for me (Qaumaniq) was that, during the entirely Hebrew service, I was able to supernaturally follow along in Hebrew. I am not Hebrew speaking so this was somewhat of a pleasant surprise to Suuqiina and me. After the service, several of the Jewish people come up to me and said, "We see that you know our prayers and songs in Hebrew, are you Jewish?" I replied, "I think that God loves you so much that He just allowed me to speak your language to honor you." They were so pleased.

Some would ask, "Why did you not take the opportunity to tell them about Jesus or explain about speaking in tongues?" The reason is because we went there to learn from them, to be listeners and not speakers, and to begin a relationship with them. We trust Yahweh with them, because they are His children, just as we are His children. Simply put, we were there to bring down a wall and build a bridge that we could both walk over and meet in the middle. The bridge was a bridge of honor, a bridge to the hearts of His chosen people. We want to be bridge builders.

Our meeting with the Jewish synagogue was such a blessing to us. We watched as they carried the Torah (The Word of God) around the room and they kissed it. What beautiful devotion! We needed them as much as they need us, maybe even more. After all, they are the olive tree into which we have been grafted.

A few weeks later, we were privileged to stand in the front of the Episcopal Church, in our full Native regalia, and welcome the Rabbi and the Priest, as they stood together in front of us. We welcomed them on to the land and Suuqiina said, "This is what could have been and this is what should have been."

We stood there, the host people of the land, the Jew and the immigrant church represented. Not only were we standing

together in the same room, but also we were actually partnering together. I (Qaumaniq) heard this scripture in my head,
"A three stranded chord cannot so easily be broken." I then
watched as the Rabbi and the Priest went and lit the
Hanukkah menorah together. Hanukkah is the "festival of
lights," a time of great miracles. What a miracle this was, the
Jewish synagogue and the Episcopal Church partnering
together in a joint Christmas/Hanukkah concert together. The
cantor led alongside the choir director while these two choirs,
Jew and Gentile, sang one another's songs in complete unity.
At the end of the concert, the Rabbi called the children, Jew
and Gentile, to gather under the talit together as the Rabbi,
the Priest, Suuqiina and Qaumaniq blessed the children. What
a privilege to participate in this wonderful celebration that all
began with something as simple as protocol.

Later we learned from the Father C. that the Rabbi called
him and said, "Father C. do you know anyone who speaks
Gaelic?" Father C. said, "Gaelic, why do you want some one
who speaks Gaelic?" The Rabbi answered, "Have you seen
what day the Purim Feast is on this year? It is on March 17th
and that is a Celtic holiday. We thought it would be great to
honor the Celtic culture by doing the feast in Gaelic." Father
C. said, "The only person that I know that speaks Gaelic is the
Roman Catholic priest." The Rabbi answered, "Do you think
that he would come?" And he did just that. The Roman
Catholic priest joined the Episcopal Church and the Reformed
Jewish Temple in celebrating the Purim Feasts and he helped
them to do it in Gaelic. This is the power of protocol.

This Episcopal Church is also partnering with the Korean
church and with First Nations in their area. The Messianic Jews

also meet at the Episcopal Church building for their prayer meetings. Oh the joys of the "one new man." If only we could humble ourselves, as this Episcopal Church has done, to prefer our minority brothers and sisters. We would all see great forward strides in the Kingdom of Yahweh.

In 1999, Suuqiina was a part of a reconciliation conference with a church in Thunder Bay, Ontario. The pastoral couple, Pastor K. and Pastor L., were gracious hosts and the conference, the first of its kind in the area, was a great success. That church, in Thunder Bay, was in the process of saving toward a new church building.

At the close of the conference, Pastor K. called his elders to one side and said to them, "I feel that the Lord is speaking something to us as a church." He continued by saying, "I believe we are to take the majority of our building fund and divide it between these First Nations Native leaders because this is the church that God is building." The elders agreed and they took the majority of their building fund and presented it to the Native leaders that day. There was not a dry eye in the group, and it was a powerful exercise of faith for this church.

In 2003, this church was able to purchase a huge building, with the remainder of the building funds, as a permanent home. The building they purchased was at a drastically reduced rate, so reduced that Pastor K. was embarrassed to make the offer. At the encouragement of the Holy Spirit, he made the offer and was shocked when they took his offer. He and the church are convinced that this was a miracle, and that the miracle came as a result of their willingness to do redemptive and restorative acts of protocol.

Warfare by Honor

In January 2000, we were in attendance at the World Christian Gathering of Indigenous People in Australia. While attending the conference, we watched as a few Anglo-Australians performed a protocol ceremony with some aboriginal native Australians. In this ceremony, the Anglo people gifted the Aboriginal people with five acres of choice property. The Anglo people confessed the sins of their forefathers toward the Aboriginal people as they made the presentation. Again, this was a redemptive and restorative act of protocol.

Recently, a church in Hopkinsville Kentucky, along with the Pastoral couple G. and M., participated in a protocol ceremony with the Cherokee Tribal Council. Pastor G. had been developing a relationship with the natives for some time before this ceremony took place. At the leading of the Holy Spirit, Pastors G. and M. found out the appraised value of the land on which their church is located. They took half of their building fund and had it converted to gold coins. At the tribal gathering, they took the coins and presented them to the Cherokee leaders of the tribal council. Pastor G. told them, "We found out that the land our church is on is worth $12,000. We are going to pay for our land twice because you were never paid once. We recognize the injustices that have been done to your people by our forefathers." As he held up one of the gold coins he said, "We are paying you in gold because this is the reason that you were sent down the Trail of Tears...gold." This powerful redemptive and restorative act of protocol resulted in a continuing relationship with these native leaders. Some of them participate on the worship team at that church.

None of these acts represent the totality of what is owed to the host peoples of the land. There is probably no way that all the land can be restored to them, and no monetary value can be placed on their suffering and the tragedies that came at the hands of the immigrants. However, we can do redemptive and restorative acts that show our humble intentions toward these people. These "random acts" of kindness release both host peoples and immigrant peoples alike.

John Dawson states that immigrant people "feel a collective guilt for what has taken place on the land concerning the host people." I will go further to say that when we present the history concerning what has taken place on the land, most people of Euro-American decent are overwhelmed. Many feel there is nothing that can be done to remedy the past. We disagree. We believe that at this

"We believe that at this hour in history, Yahweh is giving us an opportunity for a Holy Spirit 'do-over.'"

hour in history, Yahweh is giving us an opportunity for a Holy Spirit "do-over." For those who petition Yahweh for a way to make things right, He is giving them creative ways to show true repentance, through selfless prophetic and sacrificial acts.

Right now, I pray to Yahweh, that He will touch your heart concerning the host people of the land and other minority groups where you live. We are ambassadors of the King and He has commissioned us to become bridge builders in our communities and lives. We can honor people by giving to them, tangibly, in sacrificial ways and in so doing, bring restoration to their souls.

He can give you a story similar to these. You can be a radical giver, restorer, and reconciler. All it takes is a willing, open heart, and the courage to follow your heart.

Warfare by Honor

The intercessors of Ohio and Northern Kentucky have written a "Social Contract" in order to "create an atmosphere of unity, integrity, love, and trust, and to bring maximum glory to God's kingdom." It reads:

In keeping with this we will:

1. Serve each other as royalty—with dignity, warmth, compassion and brotherly love; listening attentively and respecting our differences—with Jesus as our role model.

   Yet it shall not be so among you, but whosoever desires to become great among you shall be your servant. And whoever of you desires to be first shall be servant of all. (Mark 10:42)

2. Be patient, quickly forgiving one another and preferring others above ourselves.

   Then Peter came to Him and said, "Lord, how often shall my brother sin against me, and I forgive him? Up to seven times?" Jesus said to him, "I do not say to you, up to seven times, but up to seventy times seven. (Matt. 18:21-22)

3. Respect the authority of leaders and follow them in unity and in trust. A leader is someone who sets aside their own personal agenda and takes on a greater agenda of service to others.

   Let every soul be subject to the governing authorities. For there is no authority except from God, and the authorities that exist are appointed by God. (Romans 13:1)

4. Operate with integrity, to the highest good of all, being willing to risk rejection to say the hard things—but saying them in love, being sure to speak blessings.

Let no corrupt word proceed out of your mouth, but what is good for necessary edification, that it may impart grace to the hearers. (Ephesians 4:29)

5. If a conflict or offense arises, we will prayerfully proceed according to the principles of Matthew 18.

   Moreover; if your brother sins against you, go and tell him his fault between you and him alone. If he hears you, you have gained your brother. But if he will not hear, take with you one or two more, that 'by the mouth of two or three wit - nesses every work may be established'. And if he refuses to hear them, tell it to the church. But if he refuses even to hear the church, let him be to you like a heathen and a tax col - lector. (Matt. 18:15-17)

6. We will not escalate or publicize a problem by indiscriminately discussing the issue with others.

   That they all may be one, as You, Father, are in Me and I in You, that they also may be one with Us, that the world may believe that You sent me. John 17:21

7. We promise our support for this Social Contract and commit our personal efforts to uphold it in our daily interactions.

   Love must be sincere. Hate what is evil: cling to what is good. Be devoted to one another in brotherly love. Honor one anoth - er above yourselves. Never be lacking in zeal, but keep your spiritual fervor, serving the Lord. Be joyful in hope, patient in affliction, faithful in prayer. Romans 12:9-13

(from the Transformation Cincinnati & Northern Kentucky brochure)

Formal commitments, like the one made by Transformation Cincinnati and Northern Kentucky, help people focus on the need and opportunity to become honorable and to live, actively, honorable lives. Maybe you and your family can write a "commitment to honor" for your own lives. This would be one step toward becoming people of honor.

We hope this little handbook has challenged you. This life of honor and protocol is a good life, a path of beauty. The main challenge is not the amount of things to be learned, but the ability to maintain a teachable heart. Our mutual enemy, the enemy of our souls, is doing all he can to destroy honor and every opportunity for honor to be shown. It is a very personal war but it's a war we can win. We were born with a human spirit full of honor. If that honor has somehow been displaced, make every effort to recapture it. It will be worth it.

You have honored us by reading this book. We say a hearty "Thank you and shalom!"

* The names of people have been abbreviated to allow for confidentiality

Endnotes

Introduction

1. John W. Friesen, *Sayings of the Elders* (Calgary, Alberta, Canada: Detselig Enterprises Ltd., 1998), p.58

2. Friesen, Ibid.,p.65

Chapter One—Honor

1. Fawn Parrish, *Honor —What Love looks Like* (Ventura, California: Renew, 1999), p.28

2. Gary Smalley, *The Gift of Honor* (Nashville, Tennessee: Thomas Nelson, 1987), p.16

3. Parrish, Ibid.,p.28-29

4. Ray and Elizabeth Levesque, *The Four Values of the People* (Vancouver, Canada: 1000 Tipis, 2003), p.1-2

5. Alyssa Loukota, *Protocol* (Legacy Foundation newsletter: 2001)

6. Essays by Alaska Natives, *Alaska Native Ways—What the Elders Have Taught Us* (Portland, Oregon, Graphic Arts Center Publishing:2002),p.1-139

Chapter Two—The First Step of Protocol

1. Dr. Henry Cloud & Dr. John Townsend, *Boundaries* (Grand Rapids, Michigan, Zondervan:1992), p.29-30

2. Cloud & Townsend, Ibid., p.33-34

3. Cloud & Townsend, Ibid., p.34

4. Cloud & Townsend,Ibid., p.35

5. Cloud & Townsend, Ibid., p.36

6. Cloud & Townsend, Ibid., p.36

7. Cloud & Townsend, Ibid., p.36

8. Smalley, Ibid., p.16

9. Mark Dupont, *Walking Out of Spiritual Abuse* (Kent, England, Sovereign World: 1997), p.30

10. Gary Chapman, *The Five Love Languages* (Chicago, Ill., Northfield:1995),p.14

Chapter Four—Honoring the Elders

1. Wu Siu Yan, *The Importance of Honoring the Elders* (Admirality Pacific.net, website:2002), p.1-4

2. Robert T. Kiyosaki & Sharon L. Lechter, *Rich Dad Poor Dad* (New York, New York, Warner Books: 2000), p.1-207

3. Judith Aftergut, Ruth B. Shields, Deborah London Baker, Christopher C. Jones, *Ways of Honoring* (Internet: 2004), p.1

4. Rabbi Lewis Warshauer, *Parashat B' Haalotekha* (Internet, A Taste of Torah: 2002), p.1-2

5. Administration on Aging, *Honoring Our Elders* (Title VI Programs, Internet: 2002)

6. Aftergut, Shields, Baker, Jones, Ibid., p.8

7. Andrew Flack, *TCF Funds Video Project—Honoring Penasco area Elders* (Taos, New Mexico, The Taos News: Aug. 2002), p.B11

8. Pet Therapy Inc., *Honoring Our Elders* (Internet: 2004), p.1-3

9. Patrick Dunn, *Spreading the Learning to Listen* (Albequrque, New Mexico, West Side Journal: Feb. 7, 2004), p.1

10. Elijah House News Writer, *The Wedding of Ministry: Pro -phetic and Healing* (Idaho,Elijah House Inc.: Issue 1.02, 2003), p.1-4

11. Tracy Green & Todd Temple, *52 Ways to Show Aging Parents You Care* (Nashville, TN, Thomas Nelson: 1992)

12. Frederic and Mary Ann Brussat, *Reverence is the Way of Radical Respect* (The Lutheran: Nov. 2002), p.1-2

Chapter Five—What's In a Name?

1. Norine Dresser, *Multicultural Manners* (New York, New York: John Wiley & Sons, Inc., 1996), p.153

2. Dresser, Ibid., p.153

3. Terri Morrison, Wayne A. Conaway, and George A. Borden, Ph.D., *Kiss, Bow or Shake Hands* (Holbrook, Mass.: Bob Adams, Inc., 1994), p.269

4. Morrison, Conaway, and Borden, Ibid., p.184

5. Morrison, Conaway, and Borden, Ibid., p.ix

6. Dresser, Ibid., p.154

7. Ralph Gower, *The New Manners & Customs of Bible Times* (Chicago: Moody Press, 1987), p.62

8. Kikawa, Daniel, *Perpetuated in Righteousness* (Aloha Ke Akua Publishing, 1994) p.26-27

9. Karen Liptak, *North American Indian Ceremonies* (New York, NY: Franklin Watts, 1992), p.16

10. Liptak, Ibid., p.18

11. Friesen, Ibid., p.63

Chapter Six—Rites of Passage

1. Pastor Tyrone Folsomito, *Contextualizing the Gospel: Navajo Style* (Native Reflections newsletter),p.3

2. Rico Leffanta, *Fort Apache Puberty Rite* (Internet: 2001), p.1-34

3. Father Michael Oleksa, *Girls Must Learn to Use Words Productively* (Anchorage, AK, Anchorage Daily News: July 14, 2002), p.D3

4. Karen Liptak, *North American Indian Ceremonies* (New York, NY., A First Book: 1992), p.18-19

5. John Blacket & Reggie Yates, *Chosen By God to Redeem Cultures* (Cannington, West Australia, Knesed: 2001), p.186-187

6. Patrick I. Twohy, *How Young Indians Take Their Place as Adults* (Internet, 1000 Tipis: Oct.28, 2002), p.1-2

7. Ralph Gower, *Manners and Customs of Bible Times* (Chicago, Il. Moody Press: 1987), p.63

8. Rabbi Moshe Schapairo, *What is a Bar or Bat Mitzvah?* (Internet, aish.com, Jewish Literacy: 2004), p.1-2

Chapter Seven—The Protocol of Weddings

1. Gower, Ibid., p.64-69

2. Liptak, Ibid., p.22-26

3. Leslie Gourse, *Native American Courtship and Marriage Traditions* (New York, NY., Hippcrene Books Inc.: 2000), p.61-67

4. Gourse, Ibid., p.75-79

5. Gourse, Ibid., p.81-89

6. Writer, *Indian Tribes—Marriage* (Internet, American Indian Geaneology), p.1-4

7. Basil Johnston, *Ojibwa Ceremonies* (Lincoln, Nebraska, University of Nebraska: 1990), p. 77-92

8. Rigoleerta Menchee', *I, Rigoleerta Menchee'* (Internet), p.59-78

9. Internet, *Wedding Ceremonies and Customs*

10. Robert Lam Pingfai, *Local Tradition Chinese Wedding* (Hong Kong, Japan, Hong Kong Museum of History: 1986), p.?

11. Internet, *Wedding Ceremonies and Customs*

12. Manataka American Indian Council, *The Old Cherokee Wedding* (Internet), p.265

13. The African Guide.com, *African People and Culture* (Internet), p.1

14. The African Guide, Ibid.,p.2

15. The African Guide, Ibid.,p.2

16. Art and Life in Africa, *Masai Information* (Internet)

17. The African Guide, Ibid.,p.3

18. World-weddings.net, *Destination Weddings in Pakistan* (Internet)

Chapter Eight—Grief as Honor

1. Dennis Smith, *Report From Ground Zero* (New York, NY, Penguin Group: 2002), p.256-257

2. Gail Sheehy, *Lessons of Two Tragedies* (Parade Magazine: Aug.24,2003), p.10-11

3. John and Geri GrosVenor, *NW District Church Report* (Internet: Aug.2000), p.1-3

4. Kevin Fedarko, *This Ride is About Our Future* (Parade Magazine: May 16, 2004), p.4-7

5. Tina Zarlenga, *In Memory of...How It All Began* (Internet, IMO: 2004), p.1-2

6. Church Initiative Staff Writers, *Grief Share* (Wake Forest, N.C.,Church Initiative: 1999), p.126-127

7. Church Initiative Staff Writers, Ibid., p.87

Chapter Nine—Entering Another Nation

1. Friesen, Ibid.

2. Qaumaniq and Suuqiina, *Can You Feel the Mountains Tremble? A Healing the Land Handbook* (Anchor Point, AK: Inuit Ministry Int'l., 1999), p.77

3. Suuqiina, Ibid., p.93

4. Many indigenous people are matrilineal and one is identified by his history from his female line. Generally an inherited position was identified so the host would knew and adjust the protocol accordingly.

5. The St. Louis was a ship of some 900 Jews that made its way across the Atlantic during World War II. It was turned away by the United States and then by Canada and returned to Europe. Only a few over 200 survived

the subsequent holocaust, the rest being killed in Hitler's concentration camps.

6. Friesen, Ibid., p.49

7. Friesen,Ibid., p.60

8. John Blacket and Reg Yates, *Chosen By God to Redeem Cultures* (Perth,Australia: Khesed Publishing, 2001), p.52-61 excerpts of a message by John Dawson at the World Christian Gathering on Indigenous People in 2000 at Meroo, Australia.

Chapter Thirteen—The Protocol of Elohim Concerning Israel

1. Don Finto, *Your People Shall Be My People* (Ventura, Ca., Regal: 2001), p.23-24

2. Michael Brown, *Our Hands Are Stained With Blood* (Shippensburg,Pa., Destiny Image: 1992), p.99

3. Rabbi Ted Falcon, PhD. And David Blatner, *Judaism For Dummies* (New York, NY., Hungry Minds: 2001), p.196-197

4. Stephano Assemani, *Constantine's Christian Creed* (Rome, Italy, Vatican: 1748), Orientalium at Occidentalium, Vol. 1 Page 105

5. Brown, Ibid., p.136-138

6. Finto, Ibid., p.86-88

7. Brown, Ibid., p.95-97

8. Brown, Ibid., p.10

9. Brown, Ibid., p.14-15

10. Brown, Ibid., p.89-90

11. Finto. Ibid., p.98

12. Finto, Ibid., p.179

13. Finto, Ibid., p.177-187

14. Reuven Doron, *One New Man* (Israel, Embrace Israel Ministries: 1993), p.178-185

15. Finto, Ibid., p.173

HONORING THE 4TH WORLD CHRISTIAN GATHERING ON INDIGENOUS PEOPLE

WHEREAS, representatives of the world's indigenous people have come to Hawaii to celebrate and encourage cultural expression in worship among indigenous peoples, recognizing the gifts of one another; and

WHEREAS, the WORLD CHRISTIAN GATHERING OF INDIGENOUS PEOPLES brings indigenous Christians from all over the world together to honor and acknowledge the unity and diversity they share in common under Jesus Christ and to provide an opportunity for indigenous peoples to bring an offering of praise and worship to the Lord in culturally redeemed ways; and

WHEREAS, the WORLD CHRISTIAN GATHERING OF INDIGENOUS PEOPLES, has also provided an important step to healing of past hurts and righting past wrongs; and

WHEREAS, indigenous Christians all over the world want to move from being a mission field to a mission force and bring their own people to fullness of life in Christ, spreading the Good News to the world; now, therefore,

BE IT RESOLVED by the House of Representatives of the Twenty-first Legislature of the State of Hawai'i, Regular Session of 2002, that this body hereby commends the WORLD CHRISTIAN GATHERING OF INDIGENOUS PEOPLES for its work to bring unity to indigenous peoples.

_____
Speaker of the House

_____
Sponsoring Representative

_____
Chief Clerk

United States Senate
WASHINGTON, D. C. 20510

February 7, 2003

Zion's Sake
1233 Shields Road
Newport News, Virginia 23608

GREETINGS FROM SENATOR WARNER

It is with great pleasure that I extend a warm welcome to all of you gathered at the "Healing the Land" seminar. This event, held at the World Outreach Center, is sure to be a spiritually enriching experience.

I am proud to have such a fine gathering of individuals here in the Commonwealth. Your seminar will help to build a stronger community and I send you my best wishes for its success.

With kind regards, I am

Sincerely,

John Warner

John Warner

Dear Honored Guests and Participants:

It is my privilege to welcome you to Southwest Washington and thank you for helping to make this Healing The Land Seminar a successful and inspirational event!

Having recently rededicated myself to Christ, I am learning that it is not only "OK" to pray, but that it is encouraged (if not expected) by our creator. As we ask for forgiveness, courage, wisdom and strength to be good servants, why not pray for our land?

It is my hope that the Suuqiina's prophetic message will help us better understand what a precious gift God has given us, and how we can begin to make things right.

Again, welcome, best wishes and God's blessings!

Sincerely,

Brian Hatfield
State Representative
District 19

Indigenous Messengers International
P.O.Box 339
Portland, TN 37148
615-325-4324
ndigenus@comcast.net

RE: Protocol Ceremony

Dear Protocol Participant,

Let us begin by explaining what protocol is for the Healing the Land Seminars. I.M.I. believes that the Creator gave land and authority to that land to the indigenous or host people. While most of the land has been taken or transfered throughout our history, the authority has never been recinded. I.M.I. believes in honoring the indigenous people, the community leaders (ie. mayor, city council, tribal chairs, etc.), and the spiritual leaders (ie. pastors, local ministries, etc.).

The first night of a Healing the Land Seminar is entirely devoted to protocol and relational protocol. We ask the local indigenous leadership to attend or send a representative to welcome us on to their land. We ask the local government to send a representative to welcome us to the local community. And we ask the local spiritual leaders to welcome us to the land. This provides for an honorable and viable release of authority for us to conduct our seminar while in your area. We respond by receiving the welcome and giving gifts to all the participants and their spouses.

We then teach on what protocol is, it's power, and it's potential in the life of the community and in the lives of all the people.

Please understand that those who participate in the opening protocol welcoming ceremony are not expected to have to remain for the balance of the service. The first part usually takes about 45 minutes. You would be welcome to stay but that is your choice.

In a typical protocol ceremony we have the local indigenous people introduced by the hosting seminar staff - the indigenous people are gifted by the local seminar staff - the local governemnt is introduced and gifted - the local spiritual leaders are introduced and gifted - then, in that order, they welcome us (and additional speakers if they attend) to the area. We respond and give our gifts to all these participants.

It is normal for the indigenous people to give their names, tribal affiliation, and tribal position. The same holds true for the government leadership and spiritual leadership.

This ceremony is always impressive in its dignity and honor which has been lost to our society. Many people are moved by the demonstration of submission to proper authority and what it should and could have been in America.

Thank you for participating with us in this important ceremony for the Healing the Land Seminar!

Protocol Ceremony Guidelines

1. Make a list of all ceremony participants and their spouses - please make this list available to I.M.I. as soon as possible so gifts can be prepared.

2. Contact indigenous leaders, government leaders, and spiritual leaders and see that they receive the protocol letter prepared by I.M.I. Make sure they understand what is expected of them and get a commitment to attend if possible.

The Protocol Ceremony

1. The hosting venue welcomes everyone to the seminar and gives instruction about registration, bathrooms, no taping or video-taping, etc.

2. The local indigenous leaders and their spouses are introduced, welcomed, and gifted. They remain standing at the front.

3. The local government leaders, spouses are welcomed and gifted. They remain at the front.

4. The local pastor, apostles, prophets, ministries, etc. are welcomed and gifted. They remain at the front.

5. The local indigenous leaders call for Qaumaniq and Suuqiina to come forward. We are usually at the back of the venue.

6. We approach and are welcomed by the indigenous, government, and spiritual leaders in that order.

7. We respond and give gifts to all the protocol participants.

PROTOCOL

Who to invite:

The first night of the seminar will be dedicated to Protocol and the Protocol Ceremony.

Protocol, or "Warfare by Honor", is a ceremony in which we (Suuqiina and Qaumaniq) ask to be welcomed on to the land where the seminar is being held.

Although the land was taken from the Native peoples their spiritual authority on the land has not been taken, it is still intact. Because of this we ask that the native or indigenous people (sometimes called the host people) be invited to be a major part of the ceremony. We will honor their authority as host people and honor them with gifts.

Acts 17:26 ....and He made from one man every nation of mankind to live on all the face of the earth, having determined their appointed times and the boundaries of their habitation, that they would seek God, if perhaps they might grope for Him and find Him, though He was not far from each one of us

We also ask that governmental leaders (mayor,councilmen,senator,police and firefighters) be invited as well as the spiritual leaders (pastors, prophets, apostles and all of their spouses). We will also gift these people to honor them.

Romans 13:1 Every person is to be in subjection to the governing authorities. For there is no authority except from God, and those which are established by God.

We will ask for the blessing of these 3 groups of leaders to allow us to release what the Lord has given to us in spiritual truth for your area.

While we are performing the ceremony we will also be instructing the congregation in what we are doing and the spiritual significance of the actions.

This is a powerful session and it sets into motion righteousness and honor and the spirit of the seminar. It also opens up your area to unify these 3 groups of leaders and releases them to work together in future endeavors in your community.

Providing Protocol Gifts:

You will want to provide protocol gifts for each of these leaders and their spouses. If you are gifting a couple you can either give them one gift together or two separate gifts, that is up to your discretion.

Gifts are to be gifts from the heart so they do not have to be extravagant. You can enlist your local churches and their talents to participate in the gathering of gifts. This helps everyone to be involved. The gifts can be symbolic, gifts of the resources of your area or simple gifts of the heart.

You will want to let the leaders know that they will be receiving gifts as some of them may want to bring gifts to exchange as well. Let the guest know that if they want to bring g gifts that they can but are under no obligation. Also let them know that the gifts can be very simple and inexpensive.

Please let the leaders know that they will no be under any obligation to stay for the entire meeting . Let them know that they are free to go right after the ceremony is over. Some of the native people may need to be reassured that they will not be "spiritually abused" in this process. By that I mean that they will not be required to participate in the program and have the Bible shoved down their throats. We want all the leaders to know that the purpose of the ceremony is to honor them and not to control them.

Find out what tribes were "originally" (before Indian relocation acts) in your area and make of list of them and add the tribes that are in your area now. Work to find out who the native leaders are as in Chiefs or Tribal Council Members. Find out if you have any direct descendants of historical Native Americans.

PLEASE KNOW THIS: IT DOES NOT MATTER HOW MUCH THEIR BLOOD QAUMTUM IS OR IF THEY ARE MIXED BLOOD. THIS MAY MATTER TO GOVERNMENTAL AUTHORITIES BUT SPIRITUALLY THEY HAVE JUST AS MUCH AUTHORITY IF THEY ARE OF NATIVE AMERICAN DESCENT NO MATTER THE PORTION OF BLOOD LINE.

Make a list of governmental authorities and the Pastors and spouses in your area. Begin now to contact these people to get commitments for the Protocol Ceremony. Send copies of the letters that we have provided to you and also make personal phone calls. It would be even better to meet in person if possible.

Remember to pray for doors to be opened by the Lord that no man can shut. Also remember that these are the foundational stones that you are putting in place for the whole seminar. This is a powerful tool of spiritual warfare so cover yourself accordingly.

If you will commit to work diligently on this ceremony and not allow yourself to become discouraged you will be amazed at the land that will be taken for the Kingdom of God.

A Testimony of the Positive Aspects of Protocol

It is with great excitement that I share this report of the mighty "One New Man" work God is doing in Africa. I have participated in numerous mission trips over the last few years and have not seen such favor and breakthrough as we did in Malawi, Africa. Malawi is desperately poor, destitute, and suffering under an oppressing epidemic of AIDS (over 50% of its citizens are either infected with AIDS or have full-blown AIDS). Malawi is 156,000 sq. miles of land (about the size of Virginia) and has a population of 12 million people. Malawi is known as the "Warm Heart of Africa" which was self evident in the warm smiles, greetings, and friendly salutations we received everywhere we went throughout the country

Pastor Swanie Brayboy and I left Virginia on April 23rd and after two grueling days of flying arrived to the Southern Hemisphere in Malawi, Africa. Upon our arrival we immediately departed to the Hotel in the capitol city of Lilongwe for some much-needed rest. On Monday, April 26th, our first full day in Malawi, we headed to the office of the Mayor of Lilongwe to meet with the assistant Mayor. The current Mayor was campaigning for the upcoming May 18th, 2004 National Elections in Malawi. This meeting with the Assistant Mayor began our spiritual breakthrough on this trip...let me explain.

Father has taught us so much over the last several years regarding the "One New Man" of Ephesians 2:15 and Spiritual Authority. The "One New Man" that Paul writes about in Ephesians 2:15 teaches us that all walls of division and separation between Jews and Gentiles have been removed by the blood of Yeshua. Walls and division of race, class, religion, and theology are man made and not of God. Combined with this there is a spiritual authority granted to every nation and it's leaders, There are two scriptures that explain this.

Acts 17:26-27 (CJB): "*[26]From one man he made every nation living on the entire surface of the earth, and he fixed the limits of their territories and the periods when they would flourish. [27]God did this so that people would look for him and perhaps reach out and find him although in fact, he is not far from each one of us.*"

Romans 13: l-4 (CJB): "*[1]Everyone is to obey the governing authorities. For there is no authority that is not from God, and the existing authorities have been placed where they are by God. [2]Therefore, whoever resists the authorities is resisting what God has instituted; and those who resist will bring judgment on themselves. [3]For rulers are no terror to good conduct, but to bad. Would you like to be unafraid of the per -*

son in authority? Then simply do what is good, and you will win his approval; [4]for he is God's servant, there for your ben - efit. But if you do what is wrong, be afraid! Because it is not for nothing that he holds the power of the sword; for he is God's servant, there as an avenger to punish wrongdoers."

These scriptures tell us that God has made all nations and has put their leaders in place and given them their authority and if we do what is good we have nothing to fear. Unlike missionaries in days of old, we did not enter the country to espouse American or European culture and change the people to our culture. We came only to convey a message of the "Good News" of Messiah Yeshua and His salvation. We honored the governing authorities of these countries and cities and recognized that they are there because God has placed them there and we submitted ourselves to their authority. To truly have a breakthrough in sharing the Gospel in foreign lands one must have permission to operate in those countries by the leaders of those countries. That is why we met with the Mayors of the two major cities we ministered in. Romans 13:4 states those leaders are there for our "benefit!"

We met with the Assistant Mayor of Lilongwe (sorry but I do not remember his name) before we conducted any business or meeting in the country or city. We met him at 10:00am on Tuesday, April 26th, 2004, our first full day in Malawi. Pastor Brayboy, Pastor Ngwira and I were ushered into his office and he asked how he could help us. I introduced ourselves and explained that we were ministers of the Gospel from America and that we were invited to Malawi by Pastor Ngwira. I explained to him that we had new revelation of Spiritual Authority from the two scriptures I referenced earlier. I then asked his permission to allow us to minister in his city and country and would he give us his blessing. I then presented him some gifts from America, representing our home state of Virginia and America. I then explained that we are learning about the "One New Man" and that the bride of Christ is made up of many Nations, Tribes, and Tongues. I shared that we have not come to change culture or espouse some other culture. I shared that we would only be ministering the gospel to the lost and healing the sick, and that we again desired his blessing and permission and honor him since God had placed him in his position of leadership. He received the gifts with thanks and fell silent for a long pause before he answered. He looked at us and shared that no one had every done such a thing as this before. That most missionaries boldly come into their country and do whatever they desire without permission and also attempt to change the culture of the people. He thanked us again, again, and again. He gave us blanket permission to move about the Capitol City of Lilongwe and he blessed us and our mission. He then shared that he was a Christian and that Malawi needed Yeshua if it was every going to prosper and be set free from poverty, sickness, and despair. He then took numerous pictures of us with him and blessed us again and thanked us unceasingly.

That afternoon, at our first meeting, outside the building before we even entered, Pastor Brayboy led a young Malawi Man to Yeshua at the doorway. This was a powerful example of the favor and grace that was poured upon as we were given the authority to perform ministry by the leaders of Malawi. In our 5 meetings in Lilongwe over the next week over 800 were saved and hundred were healed from Malaria, various bone disorders, tooth disorders, numerous diseases and hundreds were filled with the Holy Spirit for the first time. In our last outreach in Lilongwe on Shabbat (May 1st, 2004) Pastor Ngwira hired a well-known local worship leader and his choir. In an open field of a township of Lilongwe a temporary slab board stage was erected. A generator was rented and a PA system setup. At around 2:00pm, the worship leader and his choir began praise and worship. At approximately 4:00pm, over 2,550 people had gathered to receive God's word. Over 600 received Yeshua that day (including numerous Muslims, and hundreds more were healed and set free). We also spent several days in Blantyre, the second largest city of Malawi. Again, before conducting any ministry or meetings, we met with his Honor John Chikakwiya, Mayor of Blantyre and Governor of the Southern Province of Malawi. Mayor Chikakwiya ushered us into his office and asked us what he could do for us. I explained about spiritual authority and that we recognized his authority, that it came from God, and that we submitted ourselves to his authority as guests in his country, city and province. We gifted hi with gifts that represented America and our home state of Virginia. We then asked his permission and blessing to perform ministry and share the gospel of Messiah Yeshua to his people. I again explained that we were not there to change culture or oppress people, but rather we wanted to set them free by the blood of the Lamb, and to heal and reconcile them back to God. He paused, gave us a long, incredulous gaze then spoke strongly and with great authority. He gave us permission to move freely about the province and city and gave us permission to speak to anyone we desired and to conduct as many outreaches as we desired.

He then shared that he is an Ordained Minister and that although he understood what we were doing, he had never seen anyone do it before, especially not in Malawi. He said that he was greatly honored and that if anyone gave us any trouble we were to call him personally as we were travelling about his province as his personal guests. He then got up, picked up his chair, set it in the middle of our group, sat down, and asked us to pray for him as he needed more of Jesus to carry out his duties and for prayer for the upcoming elections! We prayed for him and the country, took several pictures with him and then he walked us back to our vehicle for one more blessing before we left. In this meeting we had with Mayor Chikakwiya there was another person present who introduced himself as Mr. Ken Williams Mhango. He is the personal assistant to his Excellency Dr. Bakili Muluzi, President of Malawi and is the National Director for orphanages and non-profit aid disbursements (what a divine appointment as we had been discussing shipping containers of aid to Malawi with Pastor Howard). Mr. Mhango made several phone calls attempting to get us an audience with Dr. Muluzi. The president was returning from meetings in South Africa and could not see us at that time but made us promise that when we return we schedule a meeting with him, as he will grant us an audience! This is testimony to the power of God's word and the great favor that is bestowed upon us when we follow His plan and order! Our meetings in Blantyre and the Southern Province city of Bangula were great successes. Over 200 were saved as Pastor Brayboy and I ministered the Word of God. In our meetings were ten Pastors, six from Malawi and four from Mozambique, Zambia, Tanzinia, and Zimbabwe. One young pastor walked all night long, over 60 kilometers to attend our meetings. What a difference it makes to be in harmony and shalom with the Kingdom of God, the Holy Spirit and the leaders of the land.

—Rabbi Eric S. Carlson

Warfare by Honor

About Healing the Land Publishing

Healing the Land Publishing, led by Directors Tony and Deborah Laidig, is a non-profit ministry organization whose mission is to promote and encourage healing and reconciliation for the historic and contemporary wounds between the Majority culture and the Native American people. One of the primary ways they accomplish this vision is through developing and publishing books and other media resources focused on presenting the Good News in ways that are culturally relevant to the Native people. Through these necessary materials, bridges of listening, dialog, and respect are built that result in true reconciliation and relationship.

By donating their time, publishing knowledge and skills to Native leaders across the United States and Canada, and by researching and taking advantage of the latest technologies in publishing, they are restoring the much-needed voice of the Native people by producing ministry materials that otherwise might never be produced.

Warfare by Honor